For Her Grace, Clue N.

Library of Congress Cataloging in Publication Data
Langone, John, 1929-
  Women who drink.

  Includes index.
  1. Alcohol and women. 2. Alcohol and
women—United States. I. Langone, Dolores
deNobrega, joint author. II. Title.
HV5137.L36   362.2′92′088042   80-11557
ISBN 0-201-04354-8
ISBN 0-201-04353-X

ISBN 0-201-04353-X-H
ISBN 0-201-04354-8-P

ABCDEFGHIJ-DO-89876543210

WHO DRINK

JOHN LANGONE
DOLORES deNOBREGA LANGONE

ADDISON-WESLEY PUBLISHING COMPANY

Reading, Massachusetts • Menlo Park, California
London • Amsterdam • Don Mills, Ontario • Sydney

Introduction

This is a book about alcohol and women, a subject that has begun to draw increasing attention if only because more women drink openly today, not in secret or in keeping with certain male-inspired standards of propriety.

No one can say for certain how many women drink, with what regularity, or how many get into trouble because of it. There is, however, general agreement that more than 50 percent of adult women drink once a month or more; that the percentage of teenage girls who drink has approached that of boys; and that there seems to be an increase in the number of women with alcohol-related problems, with estimates ranging as high as 8.5 million. (It is now generally assumed that there are between 10 million and 17 million problem drinkers in the U.S. population, and that 50 percent of these are women. For years, the estimates of women alcohol-abusers were conservative, probably because so few women entered treatment or admitted to having difficulties with alcohol.)

The fact that more women drink today than ever before in our history—the United States, incidentally, ranks 15th among 26 countries in consumption of alcoholic beverages, but third in imbibing distilled liquor—raises a number of questions that are discussed in the pages ahead. What are the social, psychological, and physical factors that play a part in the drinking behavior of women? How do women differ from men in their reasons for and patterns of drinking? In what special ways does a woman's body respond to alcohol? What unique dangers might she face because of the combination of overprescribed drugs and alcohol? What effects does a woman's drinking have on her children, her husband, her friends? What treatment approaches are best for the woman with a drinking problem? What rules should a woman follow to drink responsibly?

We do not presume to have definitive answers to all of these questions nor, for that matter, should anyone else, whether clinician, counselor, or researcher. We are, however, dedicated to the proposition that information is essential in this matter because of the many myths and misconceptions surrounding the topic. This book, we hope, provides a base of historical and current information about alcohol and drinking behavior, and it offers support to women who find themselves wondering about their drinking.

Our theme is responsible drinking for those who choose to drink, not necessarily abstinence. We do not raise the spectre of a plague of alcoholism that is destroying or threatens to destroy women and society because most people who drink do so without injuring themselves or anyone else. We are, of course, aware of the chilling facts associated with alcohol abuse— 100,000 deaths a year, billions of dollars in lost productivity and health costs, the disintegration of families—and the distinction between misuse and careful use of liquor is made throughout.

In preparing this book, we relied on many sources: medical journals, papers presented at scientific meetings, newspaper and magazine accounts, and our own interviews. The sources have been cited whenever possible or practical.

While we are grateful to all who have assisted us, our thanks should not imply that each agrees with this book's point of view. We alone are responsible for that.

Hingham, Massachusetts   J.L.
January 1980   D.deN.L.

Contents

1

Women

AND DRINK

I cannot stand, I cannot bear, to see a woman drunk. I have a secretary who goes to lunch, as they say, on Wednesdays, Thursdays, and Fridays. And when she comes back she's a totally different person. She's loud-mouthed, aggressive, uncooperative. She's a bitch. I cannot stand her, I really can't. I want to hit her. I just cannot abide the aggressiveness that women seem to exhibit when they're drinking too much. I also don't like to see women go into bars alone. . . . There is a certain stigma, still. A woman who overdrinks is inviting more trouble than a man. Right or wrong, that's the way it is. I don't ever want anyone to say about me, "God, she's half in the bag."

Susanna, 36, daughter of an alcoholic
father and an executive in a San Francisco insurance company

Woman has always drunk, sometimes surreptitiously, sometimes openly. But no matter how she has chosen to indulge, she has not had an easy time of it in our dual-standard society, especially if she drinks too much. The history of women and alcohol has been tempestuous: In early times women were scorned for drinking like men; in more recent days they took up the banner of temperance; presently, women drink with men but are still subject to disparaging attitudes.

In ancient Rome, philosopher/statesman Seneca declared caustically, "In rivalling male indulgences, [women] have also rivalled the ills to which men are heirs. They keep just as late hours, and drink just as much liquor; . . . they devise the most impossible varieties of unchastity, and in the company of men they play the part of men. . . . Because of their vices, women have ceased to deserve the privileges of their sex." The literature of that period contains allusions to laws that actually prohibited women from drinking, tales of husbands killing wives who violated those laws, and reports of women forced to kiss their male relatives to prove their lips had not touched wine. Pliny the Elder mentioned a woman who was starved to death because she stole the keys to a wine cellar.

In more recent times, Prohibition saw a similar distinction between drinking men and women. "There has always been a theory that it was possible to 'drink like a gentleman,' " observed one social commentator of the period, Margaret Culkin Banning. "Deplored though his habits might be by the more temperate, a gentleman could reach the point of complete intoxication and yet not lose his standing. Large claims have even been made that a man best shows his real nature when he is drunk. But until recently no such claim has ever been made for a lady nor similar facts admitted of her. If she drank past the point of mental and physical control, she no longer was a lady. Be her previous station high or low, she was an unfortunate creature indisputably on the down grade."[1]

On the other side of the spectrum emerged the image of woman as the fiery, hatchet-wielding foe of drink. Those in the forefront of the American Temperance Movement were strong-willed women who often had drunken, abusive husbands and who, although their attitudes were understandable, warped the true meaning of temperance—"moderation in action, thought, and feeling"—so that it came to mean total abstinence. The anti-salooners like Carrie Nation, who at the turn of the century wrecked many a barroom in Medicine Lodge, Kansas with her hatchet, did much to strengthen the ideal (or the myth) of women as foes of alcohol and guardians of morality.

This image of women shunning drink, however, quickly disappeared during Prohibition as virtually everyone—the public, law enforcement officials, even President Harding (who kept a well-stocked bar in the White House)—openly flaunted the restrictive Volstead Act that legislated the shift from wet to dry. There was plenty of alcohol, whether home-brewed beer, moonshine liquor, bathtub gin, or "the real stuff," supplied by organized crime and bootleggers. Much of this contraband was dispensed in speakeasies, local cabarets or taverns operating in an atmosphere of false secrecy (given the fact that police surveillance was quite relaxed) that catered to both men and women.

The 1920s drinking scene was aptly described by American social historian Frederick Lewis Allen: "Father may still go down to Cassidy's bar of evenings, but since prohibition mother goes down with him. Under the new regime not only the drinks were mixed, but the company as well. . . . Among well-to-do people the serving of cocktails before dinner became almost socially obligatory. Mixed parties swarmed up the curtained grilles of speakeasies and uttered the mystic password. Girls along with men stood at the speakeasy bar with one foot on the old brass rail. The late afternoon cocktail party became a new American institution."[2]

And with it all came a revolution in morals and manners and a new view of drinking that included women, a view that may well have left its mark on humankind for better or for worse. The drinking woman had burst upon the scene.

Whether out of feminist rebellion or as part of the general reaction to the attempts of misguided moralists to regulate personal habits, or simply for the fun of it, women began to do, openly, what men did.

But today, for all the efforts of women's liberation and our sophisticated approach to male/female issues, the drinking woman—and especially the woman with a drinking problem— still bears a stigma. She has won the right to drink with and like men; you'll find her on junior and senior high school campuses, in cocktail lounges, at business lunches, and in bars that were once male bastions. But she has not won the right to be regarded in the same way as men when drinking or intoxicated, or when they have finally become alcoholics.

SOCIETY'S ATTITUDE

What characterizes society's attitude toward the drinking woman? There seems to be a three-pronged approach: disgust, denial, and protection. Sometimes, just drinking at all is enough to invite disapproval—even from other women—but drunkenness in a woman elicits deep feelings of dislike, even abhorrence. After all, goes the stereotype, women must be aware of the moral consequences—not a preposterous conclusion in light of their classification as angels and heavenly things (generally by dads, rarely by theologians), and the alleged ingredients that go into their makeup (sugar, spice, and everything nice).

Contributing to the unreality are the abundant references to unsavory connections between women and drink: the Bacchanalia, drunken Roman orgies whose female devotees spent their time in abandoned inebriation, drinking copious quantities of wine and dismembering and devouring wild beasts; Belle Starr, the hard-drinking bandit queen, promiscuous and tough; and Doll Tearsheet, the violent-tempered whore of

Shakespeare's *Henry IV* whose language, when lubricated with a pint, made men blush.

Is it, then, any wonder that society must deny a woman's drinking problem; that a heavy-drinking woman is viewed as not being a "proper" or "real" woman? Should we be surprised that a woman associated with drink in any way should be considered "loose?"

Edie, 22, a bartender in a north-of-Boston bayside inn, is a perfect example of how some people view a woman who shrugs off convention, especially when it involves a drinking environment:

People say to me, "How can you do that sort of thing?" Men's attitudes are very interesting. They come in and expect that a woman behind a bar is available. You just have to know how to deal with that. I know they feel this way and it hurts me sometimes. I even get customers who will say, "Hey, waitress," and that makes me furious. I'll tell them I'm not a waitress, I'm the bartender, and no matter how many times I correct them they'll call me a waitress. My day boss—I work in an office—knows where I work nights, and every time I bring up the subject of my other job he says, "Are you going to be waitressing tonight?" I say, "Look, I'm a bartender," and he says, "Oh, don't you have trouble carrying those trays? You're not all that big," and I say, "No, no, no. I'm a bartender, I pour the drinks, I mix them, like, you know, Duffy's Tavern?" And he goes, "You mean you actually . . . ?"

And my father, that's something else. Last summer, when I was bartending six nights a week, Saturdays off, making really good money . . . my father says to me, after he sees these little secretaries in his office taking home maybe $125 a week, 9:00 to 5:00 . . . he says, "Edie, when are you going to get a real job?" Now, here I am, making twice as much as those girls he works with, and I have an ordinary day job to go with it, a "respectable" one I suppose you'd call it, and he consistently says bartending isn't a real job. When I tell him the money is good, he tells me money isn't everything. When I tell him I'm happy doing it, he says you don't meet the right kind of people in bars. He gives me the nightlife stuff, all that, says that bar girls are bar girls and people think

they're loose and easy, and I tell him that's probably true, people think-
ing that, and maybe some are, but I'm not like that. He just can't accept
it.

We seem to have a real need to reject the idea that women
could be intimately involved with drink—especially that they
could have a drinking problem—for to accept the notion would
be to accept dramatic change, and that is most difficult to do,
especially when the beliefs are practically written in stone.
Human societies are, after all, ritualistic, and the myths—when
they are challenged—die hard. So it is sometimes easier to deny
that a real and unbearable problem exists than to take the steps
to remedy or change it. To deal with the problem of women
and drink means to admit it, and a great many individuals still
cannot do that. Denial of the problem protects the blameless
image of women, protects them from being hurt by public
opinion—and "protects" women alcoholics from getting
much-needed help.

Yet another aspect of that denial might be mentioned here,
one that is closely linked to the male's image of himself. It has
been suggested that a husband who denies that his wife drinks
does so not so much to protect her as to protect himself. He
fears disclosure will reflect poorly on his masculinity: He can't
be a "real" man—he can't control his wife; he picked a loser (or,
she's all he could get); he obviously can't satisfy her. Painfully
aware that many women have "driven their husbands to drink,"
he might feel at fault—but may not be able to accept such a re-
versal of "traditional" roles. Conversely, he might remain silent
to encourage her drinking, which could afford him a sense of
moral superiority or power.

Returning to the displeasure that is often expressed over a
woman who drinks too much, it's safe to say that the same thing
doesn't apply to men. While an intoxicated man may be considered funny or even macho, he is often simply ignored: People
discount what doesn't matter, what isn't important. But a

woman drunk is always on stage, she always stands out, whether or not she wants it that way. She is violating a strong societal standard, and everyone is painfully aware of her behavior, although the outward reaction may appear minimal. (Interestingly, the alcoholic man is sometimes seen as weak, pitiful, and almost feminine, whereas the alcoholic woman is often described as hard, disagreeable, and masculine.)

Kevin, a 62-year-old bartender at a Boston hotel, has this to say about his female customers:

You can always tell a woman at the bar when she's had too much. All of a sudden, their voices raise a bit, you know? A guy, when he's had a little, is not shrill like that. And men, you can hustle them off to the men's room and straighten 'em out. . . . But a woman, Jesus Christ, who's going to take 'em to the lady's room? Nobody wants to get near a broad when she's loaded. . . .

In the old days, women were more or less honest about why they were coming in to a bar. If they were hustlers they used to come in and say, "I'm a working girl," and they never bothered anyone. But today, Jesus Christ, they bounce around in these joints and nobody knows what the hell they're up to. . . . You can't tell whether they're hustling or not anymore.

Not too long ago, women couldn't sit at a bar here, they'd have to sit at a table and we'd serve 'em there. That's the way it ought to be. When you see a woman sitting at a bar you think she's loose. It's natural that you should think that.

It's lousy today. And the crap they drink. Screwdrivers. And vodka like it's going out of style. Stuff leaves you breathless, for Chrissake, maybe that's why women sound so bad when they've had too much, all that vodka. And the Toasted Almonds. Kahlua, for Chrissake, Amaretto, and cream—equal parts, they tell me. And these women will have three apiece. That's their lunch. Three Toasteds, a slab of cheese, and a half dozen Ritz crackers. Lunchtime.

And you always have to take care of them if anything goes wrong. Like this nurse used to come in, slight-built thing, and she'd pack 'em in, screwdrivers, five, six. She'd get polluted and we'd have to call a cab for her and get her sent home. Now a guy, well for Chrissake, you just stand him up and get him the fuck out the door. None of this getting the bell-hop stuff and calling the cabbies and so on. I suppose you have to do that though . . . because it could be your daughter or your wife. . . .

Ah, the all-male bar, it's a grand idea. They'd have the law down on you if you tried it today, wouldn't they? The only women coming in in the old days were the wives [who] didn't want their men to be drinking. Or, occasionally you'd get one who'd like a nip or two herself, and that wasn't so bad because we all knew them and they didn't do it so much. They're ruining drinking in bars, these young women coming in.

The experts say that Kevin isn't alone in his views. "Although there are continuing forces in 'progressive' societies to promote the 'equality' of men and women," says the American Medical Association's *Manual on Alcoholism,* "discriminatory standards continue to be applied. In spite of our own expanding social tolerances, it is readily apparent that most of us react more strongly to a severely intoxicated woman. Such reactions may in part account for what appears to be the greater secrecy employed in women's drinking, and they illustrate the impact of gender-inspired standards."

The fact that many alcoholic women exhibit behavior patterns different from those of alcoholic men—a point to be examined in more detail later in the book—may be behind this reaction, but too often the reason for it is moralistic judgment: People cannot abide the disturbing sight of a woman drunk. As a result, we regularly hear references to the "neurotic" woman alcoholic, as opposed to the "sick" male alcoholic. These attitudes not only interfere with treatment, in terms of its availability and its approach, but they also stand in the way of responsible drinking, which should be the goal of everyone who has opted to drink.

Woman, whether single or married, is expected to be many things to the men in her life: glamorous companion, nurturing mother, meticulous housekeeper. When a professional opportunity is presented, moreover, she is expected to "know her place," which means that if she tries to succeed and sometimes overcompensates due to obstacles before her, she is "pushy," "unfeminine," "bitchy," a "women's libber," or in harsher terms, a "ball-buster."

It is no wonder that when she is unable to play the "feminine" role that society demands of her, a woman might turn to drink in an effort to dull the anxiety and guilt gnawing at her. But when she does drink, she is expected to do so "like a woman"; this added demand produces further anxiety that can and often does call for more drink. Too often a woman whose drinking habits have been caricatured as unfeminine begins drinking alone, in private, out of fear of ridicule. If she holds a sensitive professional position, her lack of control regarding alcohol may be whispered about and she may even be dismissed, while a male in a similar position is urged—even forced—by his employer to seek help. If she is black, she suffers doubly.

Even when the drinking woman, black or white, hits the skids, drinking cheap muscatel from a paper-covered bottle in an alley, she is seen by her male derelict companions as worse off than they. The skid-row woman herself often believes that she is a sorrier specimen than her male peers, and prefers to drink apart from them.

It would be quite unfair to give the impression that women alone must deal with gender-inspired standards. Men, too, have to cope with many obligations and must also try to live up to stereotypical images—lover, provider, caring father, inspiring leader—and these may often parallel those that have fallen on women. One might argue, then, that since the obligation–anxiety–drink pattern can occur in both sexes, women and men who drink too much are not, after all, very much different. To some extent this is perfectly true.

ALCOHOLIC MEN—AND THEIR WIVES

A consideration of the wives of male alcoholics also provides evidence of the way women are viewed when alcohol abuse enters their lives. The literature is virtually bursting with reports on the personality of the wives of alcoholics who are themselves maladjusted, hostile toward men, shrewish, and morally superior. Harvard psychiatrist Joseph C. Rheingold has collected what he terms a "remarkable concordance of opinion" on the wives of excessive drinkers, and it is a startling litany: The wives are "similar in terms of poor personality integration"; good adjustment is rare; they are equally in need of psychotherapy or counseling because their personality disturbances may be even more serious than their spouses'; some need to be married to weak, dependent, alcoholic men so they may play the role of powerful mother and father; they "stand to gain unconscious vicarious gratification from their husband's asocial behavior, while gaining defensive reassurance by their overt castigation of it"; they express resentment if treatment makes the men become more assertive; they feel angry, rejected, and abused if their husbands spend too much time at AA meetings.

"I have cases of wives who almost demanded that their husbands become drunkards," observes Rheingold, "[who] fostered their drinking, and who seemed to regard their sobriety as a threat. Some of these women had alcoholic fathers and unconsciously have a need to re-enact their mother's relationship with her husband.

"Other women drive their husbands to drink not only by reason of a specific wish but out of vicarious gratification of antisocial impulses, a mechanism we observed in connection with juvenile delinquency. Others are just vexatious enough to make the husband seek to drown his misery. The incessant nagging and recrimination over his drinking is so obviously an incitement that one wonders whether the wife means to achieve this end. Daughters of such women have insight into the provocativeness of their mothers and blame them for the father's drinking. Some of them recount a gradual change of personality in the father and the resort to alcohol under the mother's harrassment. When they try to moderate the mother's behavior or suggest that her handling of the problem accomplishes the opposite of the intended effect, they may meet with such vindictiveness that they are obliged to take sides with her. The eyewitness accounts of daughters—less often of sons—adds a great deal to one's insight into alcoholic men and their wives."[3]

Undoubtedly, a good deal of this sorry picture is true, and to deny that this sort of behavior exists is to contribute to the myth of woman as all-loving and ever-compassionate and humane, and to do injustice to the alcoholic men throughout history who have been angered, injured, and abused by their wives, and whose drinking has worsened because of that. But it would be just as wrong to come away with the impression that all married men with a drinking problem have acquired it because of their wives, or for that matter, that all single men who drink to excess do so because they harbor rage and hostility toward mothers who might possess traits similar to those described.

It is also difficult to determine whether some of the behavior and traits present in the wives of alcoholic men are causes or effects of the drinking. For instance, was the wife of an alcoholic poorly adjusted before she married, or did she become that way because of her husband's drinking? This same argument is offered when considering the causes of alcoholism. Does a person drink heavily because he or she is depressed or does the drinker become depressed because of the drinking?

Whatever the truth regarding the behavior of wives of alcoholic men, one thing appears certain: These women do not seem to get the sympathy that the husbands of alcoholic women get. The man with an alcoholic wife, surveys have shown, is more likely to be perceived by family and friends as a "nice man" and probably not responsible for his wife's drinking. He also appears to receive more support from his sons and daughters, who often express more negative feelings toward their mother than they would toward their father if he had the problem.

On the other side of the coin, the wife of an alcoholic will often suffer in silence, accepting and enduring her husband's drinking and sometimes even gaining strength from the experience. But such a woman may not necessarily react the same way toward her children's drinking habits. Fearful that they may follow in their father's footsteps, she might become more critical of their conduct, nagging incessantly about the evils of liquor, possibly demanding total abstinence. Daughters especially seem to bear the brunt of such criticism, either because of the mother's traditional attitudes toward women and alcohol, or perhaps because the mother is trying to form an alliance with a female member of the family who might side with the father.

Unfortunately, daughters of these women usually blame them for the father's drinking, and instead of heeding the heavy-handed messages about teetotaling or moderation in drinking, they begin using alcohol immoderately. Mary, 45, offers a woman's views of the pressures and guilt facing a woman who drinks, and the role of a mother in all of this:

I think society puts us women on pedestals. Fall off and you're through. . . . If you flunk out, that's it, you're written off. In my own life, I had a lot of that sort of thing, mostly from my mother. I really felt, for a long time, that she had me on some sort of pedestal. She was very strict, a real Catholic classic—Irish-born, worked for priests, went to church a lot—still does—down in Florida where she lives. Hated sex, I think, which is too bad. Maybe she didn't really hate it, I'm not really sure about that statement. At least she never talked about it, let me put it that way. It was always, the few times she mentioned anything like that, "Don't do it," "Save it for your husband." She must have been the second virgin who conceived. . . .

Well, she wanted me to be a nun like her sister, and she used to take me to visit her. She'd tell me what a nice little Sister of the Poor, or a Venerini Sister or a Maryknoll I was going to be some day. And I admit I used to fantasize a little about what sort of habit would be most becoming, and I knew them all. I even used to think I wanted to be a Trappistine Nun, you know, the Cistercian Nuns of the Strict Observance. God, can you see me in a cloister? A horny woman with a thirst for booze?

Later, I used to fantasize I was Molly Bloom in that Joyce novel,
Ulysses—*you know, sensual. Well, I suppose I liked the boys too much,
and in those days you had to do a lot of sneaking around. It wasn't as
easy or as acceptable as it seems today. Sex in the back seat of a car
parked along the river, under the bleachers in the high school stadium,
under the bushes. We were always looking over our shoulders, it seems.*

*I was hanging around with an older crowd then, and we'd drink
an awful lot at parties and bars. When I'd come home my mother and I
would fight like demons. She'd call me all sorts of names, whore and
bitch, sneak, drunk, you name it. She said she hoped I never got married
because I'd be an unfit mother, and she used to say I was just like my
dad, the bum, as she referred to him.*

*Yes, he was an alcoholic, and I was truly ashamed of him. He'd
come into the drugstore where I worked and he'd embarrass me—not on
purpose, I don't think; that was just his way. He was drunk. The pharmacist and the customers all knew I was his daughter. It was very
difficult for me then. . . .*

*I started to drink more after my mother's fights with me. And I felt
guilty most of the time. Just like I'm sure my dad felt. She tolerated his
drinking in the way that only an Irish mother can—long-suffering, felt
she deserved it for her sins, whatever those were. I kind of wish she had
hit the bottle, too, I really do. All she did was sigh over the table, and
over his trouble, she'd call it, and act so . . . morally superior all the
time. He was afraid of that, her moral tone, as I suppose I was, and still
am, to some extent. But the thing is, while she never really argued with
him about his drinking, just sort of accepted it and laid the guilt on him
quietly, I got it both barrels, shouting all the time.*

*It is difficult, after all, not to feel guilty when you're a woman and
your mother is forever calling you a booze-hound and a scum bag, when
all the cops know you, and the neighbors, too. And I still do feel guilty,
especially when I'm really bombed and when I think of my mother down
there, praying for me and for my father's soul, saying how could she
have gotten blessed with two like us, when is it going to end, when is her
daughter going to straighten up? Maybe it is good I didn't marry. . . .
I don't know if I could stand my husband saying those same things, or
my child feeling I was a failure, having my kid embarrassed when I
walked into the drugstore.*

Children, too, react differently to mother and father drinkers. Marion is middle-aged, married, and has a drinking problem:

> *Kids especially, I think, hold on to that image of mother as "M is for the million things she gave me, R is for the right and right she'll always be," that kind of stuff. It's nice, but it sort of makes me feel like a false idol. I remember a time—we were at this party—and I sort of started to act a little crazy, got the giggles and all that. But the interesting thing was I hadn't had a drop to drink that time. You know, I do like to raise the devil a little now and then and sing a lot of the old songs, and I was having a great old time. Got up and did a belly dance on a table, really got into it. And you know what? One of my kids was there, 17 years old, and when I sat down she said, "Hey Ma, how much have you been drinking, anyway?" She said, "You always act so stupid when you're drinking."*
>
> *Now here's a kid smokes dope, drinks beer down on the beach, and goes out with the guys who've always got the wine in a paper bag—can't do without it, the little toads. And here's a kid never opens her mouth when Dad comes home with a load on, or runs over the flower bed with the car at 2 A.M. "Oh, that dad," she said the time he did that, "Oh, that crazy dad, what a nut." But me, Mom, I get the Judgment Day routine. . . . And it does hurt. I remember after she said that about my acting stupid, I really beat myself up that night, telling myself that if she felt that way I'd really better watch it those times I do drink. Sort of reminded me of that old song, you ever hear it? ". . . She was a wild and lovely rose, a party life was all she chose. . . ." And here's the punch line: "The years had left their mark, her eyes had lost their spark, she's just a painted, tainted rose. . . ." You can't forget that kind of stuff if you've got a kid.*

"PROTECTIVE" TREATMENT

There is a tendency to ignore the fact that, when any person drinks uncontrollably, she or he is expressing some personal disorganization, and the various labels applied, along with the denial that women can be alcoholics, are not only unfair and inaccurate but tend to affect the way treatment is suggested and practiced. Physicians, for example, have been notoriously reluctant to place alcoholic women in treatment centers, and in this they have been aided and abetted by male members of the drinking women's families. One study, in fact, found that only one out of ten alcoholic women mentioned a doctor as being involved in motivating them to visit a treatment center, a classic example of the male's traditional view of woman and of his own role as her protector, as the person who must "save" her from the stigma of alcoholism that might accompany involvement in a formal treatment program.

So what do they do, some of these "protectors"? They prescribe tranquilizers on the assumption that an underlying anxiety is behind the drinking. There are times, of course, when tranquilizers are appropriate, as when some psychiatric disorder accompanies the drinking, or when the alcoholic is facing a major crisis. However, they generally should not be prescribed casually because they can produce dependence—a situation akin to taking away an alcoholic's bourbon and substituting gin.

Male alcoholics are not so protected—physicians, employers, and police can and do serve as positive forces to interrupt destructive drinking behavior. But the woman drinker gets little of this help. It is almost as though there is a conspiracy of silence, of denial, whenever a woman with a drinking problem arrives on the scene. There are difficulties enough in the denial that most alcoholics themselves express when confronted about their behavior. Those persons in contact with a woman alcoholic often won't mention her drinking problem at all, subscribers to the "slip of the lip will sink a ship" notion.

Bonnie-Jean Kimball at Hazelden singles out several of those responsible for the cover-up:
•   Judges and lawyers who want to get rid of this woman as quickly as possible.
•   The social worker "system" and its personnel, who would

rather designate the problem as psychological, emotional, or familial. "They can get lost in their advocacy roles," says Kimball.

•   Marital and alcoholism counselors, many of whom prefer to deal with other issues and ignore the primary illness of alcoholism or drug dependence when it relates to the woman.

•   Sisters in a religious community who often regard alcoholism afflicting one of their own as completely unbelievable.

•   School personnel who often see the "symptom bearer," the child, but are unwilling to go to the source of the problem, the mother.

•   Employers, many of whom shield the woman and deny drug dependence.

•   Bartenders who believe they are extending sympathy to a woman customer when in fact they, like all the others who protect, are lengthening her drug-taking period.

•   Drinking friends, often the last to point the finger because, as Kimball remarks, "someone might return the favor."[4]

The police, too, often go out of their way to shield a drinking woman. Although the state trooper or patrolman who flags down a woman driver only to let her go may have the best of intentions, he not only is perpetuating her dependency but is doing no service to the public, which is menaced by a dangerous driver. As far as many officers are concerned, driving after drinking is a predominantly male phenomenon. This was demonstrated by a 1976 study that examined the social characteristics and the circumstances of arrest of seventy-three women charged with driving while intoxicated (DWI).

According to Dr. Milton Argeriou and Donna Paulino of the Services for Traffic Safety Project of Boston, a woman who is apprehended for driving while under the influence is likely to be released unless she is guilty of an additional provocation, such as involvement in an accident or verbal abuse of the police officer. Of the arrests studied, twenty-five were the consequence of weaving or erratic driving, nine were for traffic violations, and thirty-nine for accidents. In twenty-one of the arrests, the woman physically or verbally abused the arresting officer. In all, fifty-three of the same DWI arrests, over 72 percent, were associated with a traffic accident, compared to 35 percent of male DWI arrests.

"The inequitable treatment of men and women by the police," the researchers reported, "while apparently favorable to women in the short run, may well be deleterious if it results in aiding problem-drinking women to keep their problem hidden."[5]

The revulsion that society directs at the drinking woman is harmful enough in terms of what it does to her self-esteem, and stands as a formidable barrier by itself to achieving equality of the sexes. But add in the other prejudicial elements, denial and protection, and the woman who drinks starts out with three strikes against her, a handicap which few men who lift a glass are ever awarded.

Shielding women who have a drinking problem, denying that they can be so troubled, can only reinforce the myths and misconceptions that have long swirled about the woman drinker. Masking the reality of the situation postpones treatment and not only prolongs her drinking habit but prevents counselors, researchers, and clinicians from learning the true facts about female drinking patterns and the reasons behind them. We'll look at some of those next.

2

WOMEN DRINK

I had a lot of friends and boyfriends, but I never felt I was good enough. I was a compulsive people-pleaser. Basically, I could never relax—and booze let me relax and be me.
Julie, a legal secretary

In any field there is contradictory research, biased samples, poorly designed and administered surveys, murky conclusions. The study of women and alcohol seems to be especially afflicted with contradictory and unenlightening research. There are reams of information and statistics, but little insight into the personal and social implications of the research.

One of the first keys to understanding the link between women and alcohol is to determine why women drink. Are those reasons substantially different from the reasons men drink and drink to excess? A number of researchers feel that the question is best answered in the negative; that the very same hereditary and environmental factors working in men can and do work in women; that the symptoms of alcoholism are identical in the two sexes; and that, therefore, problem drinking is problem drinking. Searching for the different reasons that motivate women and men drinkers, says this line of reasoning, is as fruitless as searching for definitive causes of alcoholism in general.

There seems to be little disagreement that there is no *typical* problem-drinking woman, just as there is no typical problem-drinking man. While it is true, say, that the housewife does often sip alone, she is not the only type of alcoholic to represent her sex, and generalizing from that stereotype—or from any of the others associated with women drinkers—is as unfair as generalizing about men.

However, worse in our mind is applying the assumptions about male problem drinking to women, for we believe strongly that although *some* women may drink for the same reasons that *some* men do, there is enough combination of evidence and common sense to justify the argument that women drink, for the most part, because of a psychosocial makeup that is distinct from man's.

Many elements go into the psychosocial development of a woman, factors and forces that range from her basic self-image to genetically inherited tendencies to day-to-day shifts in mood. Some of these forces, such as social or economic background, are beyond a woman's control. Others, such as life changes or stressful events, will affect different women in widely different manners. For some women, losing a job may have a relatively benign effect, for example, whereas for others it may be traumatic and may act as a catalyst to a drinking problem.

Women don't drink for one reason alone. We're going to examine several of the most prevalent forces behind women's drinking—lack of self-esteem, stress, hereditary and environmental influences, and social and cultural forces—but anyone involved in human behavior knows the difficulty in trying to analyze the complexities behind any neurosis or sickness. And while we can say firmly that there is no typical female drinker, we can use the best research available to create a composite picture. One of the things this composite tells us, reinforcing what we said earlier, is that men and women differ in their reasons for turning to drink.

Dr. Edith S. Gomberg of the University of Michigan's School of Social Work feels that men and women lead different lives, diverging sharply at adolescence. Therefore, their patterns of alcohol usage and their consequences show more differences than similarities. What are these differences and how do they make some women more vulnerable to alcoholism than others? Let's start with the biggest and most potentially damaging force: low self-esteem.

LACK OF SELF-ESTEEM

We all have difficulties at times with our self-image—call it self-esteem, if you wish—but women probably experience pangs of self-doubt a bit more often than men do. Sex-role stereotypes still exist, and women's dependency on men is continually reinforced, thus diminishing woman's self-image. We still characterize women at home, men at work despite the fact that more than 50 percent of American families are single households in which the woman is both provider (worker) and parent, and despite a 1977 U.S. Department of Labor report that proclaimed: "The concept of a family where the husband is the only breadwinner, the wife is the homemaker out of the labor force, and there are two children may be a useful one for many illustrative purposes, but it does not represent the typical American family of the mid-70s. Among husband-wife families in 1975, only 7 out of 100 fit this description."

Since the traditional roles society has defined for women and men produce quite different behavior, goals, self-images, and life experiences, women have a number of common problems that are not relevant to men. From childhood, women have been taught that as the "second sex," they are expected to derive their sense of self-worth primarily from relationships with men, rather than from achievements and activities of their own. Until recently, women were rarely encouraged to develop as independent persons with strong, secure identities. Regardless of what women do with their lives, they cannot escape society's judgment that, on some very basic level, they are inadequate simply because they are women.

Career counselor Alené Moris, who is director and cofounder of the Individual Development Center in Seattle, says that it's easy to understand why women are devalued in life, and especially in the work force. "Women have been reared to think we're supposed to turn our lives over to men," she says, "but then the funny twist comes in: Because we devote our lives to our mates, we also give them the tremendous responsibility for keeping us happy. Women must learn that the responsibility for their happiness lies in themselves."[1] She has noticed, too, that this devaluation is not something that only men practice. Moris' experience has been that often men will accept women in the work force more readily than other women do. The devaluation is inbred; it's not unusual for women to regard women as lower than men, a trait that only enhances a woman's low self-esteem. Women also are taught to compete with other women instead of being supportive, and these lessons, Moris says, instilled over many years, are hard to unlearn.

As an example, look at women's relationship to the health care system. Advertisements on radio and television, in newspapers and magazines tell us that women are less healthy than men. For years, it is true, there have been consistent reports that, although men have higher mortality rates, women experience higher morbidity—that is, more women are sick than men. Other studies have suggested that more women than men become mentally ill, as well.

According to Dr. Myrna M. Weissman, who directs the depression unit at Yale University School of Medicine, women significantly outnumber men in the frequency with which treatment for neurotic depression—which often figures in alcoholism—is sought. Dr. Weissman reported recently that a review covering forty years and thirty countries showed that there were 175 women hospitalized for depression for every man. On an outpatient basis, there were 238 women for every 100 men. None of the data on physiological and social factors that might explain why the disparity exists are conclusive, although Dr. Weissman feels that social factors, principally the difficulties inherent in being a woman, may be implicated in two ways. One may be the helplessness many women adopt; the other may be that women often see themselves as being lower on the social scale. Since they cannot achieve mastery of their lives, their self-esteem drops.

The modern woman, especially the working woman, must also face the pressures of conforming to society's expectations. Dr. Doreen E. Schecter, assistant clinical professor of psychiatry at Albert Einstein College of Medicine, has described the mental health implications of women in the labor force:

"The pressure on women today to fit into the prescriptive formula for 'making it' on all fronts—in a demanding career, as the perfect mother, wife, homemaker—is being marketed with expertise and insidious success. And American women are pathetically conforming.

"In this 'age of enlightenment,' American women are being brainwashed by the self-styled enlighteners. Identities are handed out as a matter of course. Women are told what they ought to be doing with just about every moment of their time. They are instructed why they ought to be parcelling out their lives in carefully divided segments. They are being reassured that all the wonderful goodies of life are available to them—if they follow this particular six-week course, or that particular series of rap sessions, or the other's brand of therapy.

"Reshaping an old-fashioned, outdated woman into a

slicker, trickier model with replaceable parts and other options has become a thriving business on the current cultural exchange. The dumb blonde has lost her market value to the brainy, with-it, career-oriented woman, capable of performing a few dozen activities during the course of a day with a few dozen people.

"This model of the successful woman is truly frightening. She is the ultimate in the dehumanized, depersonalized part-object, who defends against her vulnerability via detachment and numbness to any real emotion. Momentary sexual sensation with interchangeable partners is as far as she will risk it. She maintains a cheerful façade as she switches from one pseudoidentity to another, but for many women this brutalizing life-style fragments to the point where they are totally shattered. There remains no sense of self, no core, just bits and pieces of a jigsaw puzzle that no longer fit. An increasing number of high-pressured career women fit this description. They look like battered remnants of human beings. They have performed as robots for so long that when they break down they experience sheer terror. As one patient explained, 'When you've been on automatic for so long, you don't know how to operate on manual.'

"The lives of women attempting to live up to the current cultural ego-ideal have become juggling acts, competitive juggling acts at that, with many women seemingly caught up in the competition to keep ever more events, objects, people, and careers in the air. What is the point of all this? Is it a measure of success to function as a programmed robot? Is it to be overlooked that, to successfully carry off this automatic identity-switching, a woman no longer knows what it is to be or feel like a human being?"[2]

Closely tied to a woman's need to achieve the Superwoman goals of this age is a need to still feel like a woman, to be more feminine. Sometimes drink helps women achieve this. In a 1973 study, Dr. Sharon C. Wilsnack, of the Clinical Psychology Service of the Massachusetts Mental Health Center and the Harvard Medical School, reported that while men often drink to feel a sense of power, women do so to achieve a sense of womanliness. Female subjects in her study said they felt warm, loving, considerate, expressive, open, affectionate, sexy, and feminine when drinking.

Wilsnack's profile of an alcoholic shows that she experiences chronic doubts about her adequacy as a woman. These doubts arise in part from inadequate feminine identification on an unconscious level, and they may be enhanced by acute threats to her sense of feminine adequacy, such as marital problems, a miscarriage, or children leaving home. The potential alcoholic does not consciously reject her identity as a woman; rather, she consciously values traditional female roles. She may manage to cope with her fragile sense of feminine adequacy for a number of years, but when some new threat severely exacerbates her self-doubts, she turns to alcohol in an attempt to gain artificial feelings of womanliness.

"Her excessive drinking may then begin a vicious cycle, culminating in the alcoholic's characteristic loss of control over her drinking," says Wilsnack. "Although she is trying, via alcohol, to feel more womanly, the typical consequences of heavy drinking—neglect of appearance, reduced ability to cope with the demands of home and family, disapproval of family and friends—eventually make her feel *less* of a woman. These new threats to her sense of feminine adequacy cause her to drink even more heavily, until her nondrinking alternatives for feeling womanly are severely restricted and she becomes completely dependent on alcohol."[3]

Wilsnack points out that an alternative possibility is that the sex-role identity conflict fits only certain types of alcoholic women. There may be a subgroup of female problem drinkers, for example, whose "masculine identification" is complete—

that is, they consciously reject female roles and adopt a relatively unconflicted masculine life-style. Such women may drink for the same reasons men do.

"The excessive drinker," wrote Dr. David C. McClelland of Harvard a few years ago, "is the man with an excessive need for personal power who has chosen drinking as the way to accentuate his feeling of power." As men drink, their thoughts of power increase, but, McClelland added, there was no substantiation for the widely held psychiatric belief that drinking is accompanied by oral gratification or dependency fantasies.

"What did increase regularly with drinking were power thoughts, thoughts of having impact on others, of aggression, of sexual conquest, of being big, strong and influential," he said. It became apparent, Dr. McClelland noted, that power thoughts took two forms: S-power, or the desire to have power to help others, and P-power, the desire for power to dominate others.

Dr. McClelland studied university fraternity men and found that after two or three cocktails, S-power thoughts predominate in fantasies. "A person thinks more about power, but in a relatively controlled way," he reported. "After heavier drinking, say six cocktails, fear-anxiety thoughts decrease and so do thoughts about time—being on time, worry over being late, and so forth. We take this to mean that the person is becoming less reality-oriented and less inhibited, but this effect appears only after fairly heavy drinking. As one becomes less inhibited, a less controlled type of power concern dominates his thinking. S-power thoughts drop out, and P-power thoughts predominate."[4]

All of these psychological fears—the fear of failing, of appearing unfeminine—are tied to a woman's self-esteem: If she fails at what society has determined to be important (or what she perceives as important), she has failed as a woman. And sometimes alcohol helps blot out that failure.

STRESS

Virtually everyone studying women and alcohol agrees
that stressful life events are more apt to be reported as playing a
role in problem drinking for women than for men. These
events, which the women themselves mention over and over,
include divorce, abortion, dysmenorrhea, death of a parent or
spouse, alcoholism or mental illness in the family, desertion by a
lover, menopause, and the empty nest. Men, on the other hand,
are more apt to cite problems with their jobs as reasons for
their drinking. Researchers have also turned up evidence that
a large proportion of female alcoholic patients had dominant
mothers and alcoholic fathers, as well as a higher frequency of
alcoholism among relatives than do alcoholic men. As far as divorce is concerned, women alcoholics experience more divorces
than male alcoholics, generally as a result of their being de-
serted by their husbands. It's been said that nine in ten men
leave alcoholic wives, but only one in ten women leave drinking
husbands. These stressful experiences, often occurring in early
life, are obviously associated with loneliness and isolation, both
precipitating factors in problem drinking.

It may be, says Wilsnack, that the impact of external events
on women's drinking problems is a true sex difference. If so,
perhaps changes in interpersonal relationships and life circumstances may also have more of an effect in women's recovery
from alcoholism. However, she points out, it also seems possible
that because of the greater stigma of alcoholism for women,
alcoholic women may feel more of a need to explain or
rationalize their drinking in terms of events and circumstances
external to themselves. Just because a woman blames a life crisis
for her drinking doesn't necessarily prove a causal relationship.

Many problem-drinking women are depressed. According
to the surveys, they suffer more frequently from depression,
suicidal threats, delusions, and severe anxiety. Since what we

call alcoholism may be a symptom of an underlying emotional disorder as well as a disorder in itself, the real reason for the drinking may not be one of these tangible life crises but an underlying tendency toward depression over which the alcoholism is superimposed. Her problem, thus, would be independent of the drinking.

Of the stresses facing women, Edith Gomberg has this to say: "We believe that there is a sequence of events and responses which makes for a high degree of vulnerability or proneness to alcoholism. Each life experience has made for an adolescence characterized by isolation, difficulty in accepting healthy dependency relationships, depressed feelings, and unpredictable impulsivity. In this upheaval, the vulnerable young woman turns toward love and marriage with its promise of happiness, expectations which cannot possibly be fulfilled. Frustration in marriage, a low degree of frustration tolerance and of impulse control make a combination which leads to trouble. Alcohol appears as a kind of magic substance which dims the sharpness of conflict, and the multiple reinforcements of alcohol for this woman become apparent: drinking is pretty much subject to one's own control; alcohol is available; it permits one to express hostility toward others and self-contempt, too; it is escape, fantasies of female happiness, a balm for psychic pain."[5]

Indeed, marital disputes and divorce are probably the most frequently reported stresses. Yale's Dr. Weissman has said there is some evidence suggesting that marriage seems to protect men from depression, but puts women at risk. Why this seems to be so is not known. It is true, though, that marital disputes are the most common problem discussed by depressed women in psychotherapy. Divorce, too, with its accompanying pressures of loss of role as a wife, change in financial status, outside work, and the difficulties of raising children alone, increases the risk of depression in women. Dr. Weissman points out also that moving because of the husband's employment and the subsequent loss of supportive friends and family often plays a key role as well. The mobile wife must often defer her own career or take a more menial position simply to earn extra money, and these accommodations, especially if they recur with each new move, may put unbearable pressure on a wife who is always denied fulfilling employment.

Middle age, too, holds a number of medically-related problems for women, alcoholism and other drug dependencies among them. A time of review, midlife for the woman is the end of one chapter in her life story. Dr. Harvey Prosen, head of the psychiatry department at the University of Manitoba, has suggested that menopause and adolescence are similar because both are periods of great emotional stress, of conflicts about body image, or hormonal fluctuations, of aggression and ambivalence about self-control. At a recent annual meeting of the Canadian Psychiatric Association, Dr. Prosen called attention to the occurrence of promiscuity among menopausal women which, though rare, often represents a resurgence of adolescent sexual problems. For the most part, he said, these women have not been promiscuous all their lives but only during the earlier period of their adolescence. "One will usually find a situation in which the promiscuity represents a sense of alienation and failure, with anger directed inwardly and the disappointment in herself projected outwardly, producing hostility in some cases towards a marital partner who may not be an adequate partner, but further blaming him for her failure to meet her own ambitions," Dr. Prosen said.[6]

Sometimes, a woman's promiscuity after the menopause is confined to sexual relations with younger men, as she tries to prove that she is still sexually attractive. Often, too, promiscuity after menopause or preoccupation with sexual thoughts, can be seen as a reaction to how a woman feels about her role compared to a man's. "Wouldn't it be nice to be a man and be able to love them and leave them," said one woman patient.

There is little question that such behavior could signal a

period of depression that in turn could lead to dependency on alcohol, either as a substitute for unfulfilled sex or to soften the guilt that promiscuity or an extra-marital affair can cause.

Another difficulty facing middle-aged women is the price they must pay for their longevity—grief. A process involving disorganization and, ultimately, acceptance, grief lasts anywhere from four to eight weeks. It may, however, be delayed, coming on months or years later, or it can recur on anniversaries of the death, and the depression it may bring can be overwhelming.

Clinicians have known for some time that grief can cause several physical and emotional reactions, especially if the grief reaction is badly resolved. Says Dr. Melvin J. Krant, medical director of the Palliative Care Service, University of Massachusetts Medical Center, Worcester, Massachusetts: "Physical disorders such as asthma, ulcerative colitis, rheumatoid arthritis, cancer, leukemia and many others have been reported as developing as a late consequence of a grief reaction. Certainly, there is little doubt that many psychiatric diseases, especially in the affective disorders, as manic depressive psychosis and psychoneuroses, have been reported as frequent in patients undergoing early maternal or paternal losses than in control populations. The field of suicide constantly warns us to be aware of somebody who has suffered loss that has not been resolved, for such individuals are highly at risk for committing suicide. Juvenile delinquency, school dropouts, drug abuse, are all seen as having a high order of frequency resulting from loss and abandonment reactions."[7]

When raising this issue of the impact of stress on drinking, the name of Joan Kennedy—the "Golden Girl" from Manhattanville College, the former model and beauty contestant, and the wife of Senator Edward M. Kennedy—must come to mind. For a long time, her friends had whispered about her problems with alcohol, and in 1974 the newspapers began to allude to it. "Joan Kennedy Hospitalized for Complete Rest," said one headline; "Joan in Hospital for Treatment," read another. The stories did not mention alcohol, only such phrases as "emotional strain," "exhaustion brought on by a recent trip to the Soviet Union," "physical fatigue." When she attended one Washington party after a three-week stay at a New England sanitarium, the *Washington Post* reported, "Joan Kennedy, relaxed but reticent, was the center of attention at the Kennedy Center's cast party Monday night even though actress Tammy Grimes was the star of the show. . . . Half jokingly, she hid behind George Stevens, Jr., the American Film Institute's director, and Kennedy, when a reporter appeared."

Four months later, the headlines were bolder: "Kennedy Wife Faces Auto Charge." The stories referred to her driving while under the influence of liquor and crashing her convertible into the back of a car that had stopped for a traffic light in Fairfax, Virginia. On November 6, 1974, she pleaded guilty to the charge, was fined $200, and had her license to drive suspended for six months.

Although she has never publicly blamed anyone or any event for her drinking problems, to which she admitted in 1978 in a national magazine article, Mrs. Kennedy has indicated that a number of disappointments during her marriage, along with other difficulties, contributed to her drinking. "It's strange," she has said, "but for some reason, in times of crisis and expectation I could rise to the occasion and not take a drink. But then the show is over, and you are left with no goal to go back to and you feel desperately let down and unneeded."

And there *were* crises, more than most women will experience. Three miscarriages. Two brothers-in-law assassinated. A plane crash that hospitalized her husband for eight months. There was the 1969 Chappaquiddick accident. Joan recalls, "I was five months' pregnant at the time and that was another disappointment. After that, I just thought we'd tried hard enough. After all, we had three wonderful children." She stuck by her husband all during the outrage over the incident.

There was the removal in 1973 of her 12-year-old son's leg to halt the spread of cancer. "I didn't take a drink," Joan said. "I was in okay shape while he was in the hospital. I was the mother by the bedside. But as soon as he was well and back to school, I just collapsed. I needed some relief from having to be so damn brave all the time."

There was also the 1976 death of her mother, Virginia Bennett. She had died alone, of an inflamed heart muscle brought on by bronchial pneumonia, and her body wasn't discovered for some time.

And there were always persistent rumors about the senator and other women. "People ask whether the newspaper stories about Ted and girls hurt my feelings. Of course they hurt my feelings. They went to the heart of my self-esteem. I began thinking, 'Well, maybe I'm just not attractive enough or attractive any more.' . . . and it was awfully easy to say then, 'Well, after all, you know, if that's the way it is, I might as well have a drink.'"

And there was, finally, the haunting fear of Ted's running for the presidency. "A nightmare," she said once. "I worry all the time about whether Ted will be shot like Jack and Robert."

Early in 1979, she admitted that her marriage was "in limbo," and to a question about politics, she replied, "There are more important things that I've got to do for myself." By summertime, a London gossip columnist had reported an affair between Joan and a member of Parliament.

Today, things seem to have turned around for her. She is a graduate student in music at Lesley College in Boston. She attends AA meetings and talks openly about it: "I go to AA in Boston and it's wonderful. I can walk in, and there's no big flutter or whatever and I'm just like any other person who is an alcoholic and who needs help to stay sober." She has seen a psychiatrist three times a week, "working out certain things I really couldn't work out with my husband or a friend."

And when her husband announced his candidacy for the

Democratic nomination for president, she took the microphone at Faneuil Hall in Boston and told a cheering crowd: "I believe the question was will I campaign for my husband. I *will* campaign for my husband. I look forward to campaigning for him. Not only that, I look forward very enthusiastically to my husband's being a candidate, and then being president of the United States."[8]

HEREDITY AND ENVIRONMENTAL INFLUENCES

Let's turn now to some of the so-called medical causes, including theories dealing with heredity, hormone balances, and brain dysfunction, and environmental causes, including learned behavior. For our purposes we will confine our discussion of the medical model to genetics, which is the study of variation, of the differences that are passed along through generations. It is a complex science, but a highly ordered one, broad-ranging enough to play a major role in such diverse characteristics as the color of our hair and eyes as well as the tone of our emotions.

Inherited disorders such as hemophilia are passed on through the genes from parents to offspring. Some individuals also inherit at birth a *tendency* toward a certain disease rather than the actual disorder, thus beginning life with a built-in defect that makes them vulnerable. For instance, you don't inherit an allergic reaction such as hay fever. You may, however, be born with a predisposition to become allergic, especially if both your parents are allergic or if there is allergy on both sides of your family. Diabetes is usually due, also, to an inherited tendency.

Increasing attention is being paid today to heredity, brain chemicals, and brain defects in a wide variety of disorders, from schizophrenia to cancer to alcoholism. Although the role of our genes in passing on the latter is hotly debated and no definite conclusions have yet been drawn, it is known that alcoholism does occur quite often in the children of alcoholics. Dr. Gilbert S. Omenn, Jr., a geneticist at the University of Washington in Seattle, has estimated that, statistically, if one parent is an alcoholic, a child has a 10- to 20-percent chance of developing a serious drinking problem. If both parents are alcoholics, the risk increases to 30 percent. Other studies suggest that the lifetime risk of the sons of alcoholic males becoming alcoholic themselves is as high as 50 percent.

Years ago, Dr. E. M. Jellinek, the noted authority on alcoholism, reported that 52 percent of 4,372 alcoholics he studied had an alcoholic parent. In 1973, an American–Danish research team led by Dr. Donald Goodwin, then a psychiatrist at Washington University, studied 55 men who had been separated from their biological parents during early infancy. Each of the men, who were adopted by nonrelatives, had at least one biological parent suffering from alcoholism. Goodwin and his colleagues compared these men with 78 other adopted men whose parents had no known history of problem drinking and found that "significantly more"—nearly four times more—of the first group had a history of drinking problems and psychiatric treatment.

But while the notion that alcoholism runs in families can be demonstrated statistically, the way it all comes about is not understood. There are many theories about the mechanism. Jellinek believed that direct hereditary transmission of alcoholism does not occur, but that some individuals inherit a liability for developing certain frailties that can take the form of alcoholism. In a sense, this would be akin to developing a predisposition to an allergy. The drinker has inherited a certain makeup, a weak constitution, that makes her or him susceptible to the lure of alcohol. Such a theory discounts an "alcoholic gene" that might actually carry the disorder through generations.

An inherited biochemical defect could alter brain chemicals just enough to create changes in temperament that, in turn, could make one ripe for alcoholism. On the other hand, the inherited metabolic flaw might actually make an individual biologically intolerant of alcohol. It is known, for example, that Orientals are generally able to drink only small amounts of liquor—sometimes only one drink is enough to bring on a flushing reaction—before becoming ill. The reason for the reaction is an inherited gene for an enzyme that breaks down alcohol faster in individuals of Oriental blood than in others.

While the flushing mechanism and other inherited intolerances to alcohol—some of which are peculiar to women because of female metabolism, hormones, and body weight—may mean that some individuals cannot drink enough to become drunk, there is the equal possibility that some hidden and inherited factor might cause opposite effects. One theory is a dietary deficiency, caused by an inherited lack of the enzymes that metabolize essential nutrients, notably the B vitamins. This deficiency, some scientists believe, causes a craving for alcohol, a state that has actually been induced in laboratory animals. In one study, researchers deprived rats of vitamin B and discovered that when the animals were offered water or alcohol, they chose the alcohol as a substitute for the necessary energy source.

In the last analysis, the nature of the genetic factor—if there is one—that may put one at risk of developing an alcohol problem is not known. But the studies of the offspring of alcoholic parents, including twins and adopted children, and the differences in alcohol metabolism among racial groups, along with strong evidence that genetic factors predispose individuals to manic-depressive psychosis, suicide, and schizophrenia, are strong indications that heredity is a factor to be reckoned with in alcoholism. Hard-liners of the biological school accept the fact that nonphysiological factors are important, but maintain that their role is not dominant; that is, they argue that if no specific physical factors are involved, such things as emotional needs will not, by themselves, bring on alcoholism.

Whether or not heredity has a larger role than upbringing remains to be seen. But, as Harvard Medical School researchers Jack H. Mendelson and Nancy K. Mello recently pointed out, "alcoholism in the biologic parent appears to be a more reliable predictor of alcoholism in the children than any other environmental factor examined. Although the studies do not demonstrate an invariant role of genetic factors in alcoholism, the importance of further intensive study of the biogenetic basis of one subgroup of alcoholics is clearly indicated. . . . Although parental and peer influence are probably very important in the genesis of alcoholism, there is new evidence that genetic factors may be as potent as psychological and social determinants."[9]

However, while biogenetic factors are involved in the development of alcoholism and can be used to predict who may be at greater risk, this does not mean that the hereditary elements work alone. There is, as we know, a complex mix of hereditary and psychosocial ingredients in all of human nature, and it would be foolhardy to argue that the two do not depend on each other more often than not.

It is entirely possible that a meshing of nature and nurture is at work in those situations in which problem drinking "runs" in families. There is no question that brain chemicals are involved in fluctuations of mood, that depressive disorders, for instance, may be linked to an inherited deficiency of the hormone norepinephrine. Studies have shown, in fact, that if one family member suffers from depression, others in the family are more likely to be vulnerable to it. Uniting a depressive personality and a drinking environnent, or an environment that is socially deprived or unstable or unhappy, could be a lethal combination, as numerous researchers have demonstrated. This is especially important when discussing the drinking behavior of women who, as was suggested earlier, have to cope with so many conflicts. Some studies have reported, in fact, that relatively more female than male alcoholics were raised in homes in which problem drinking was an established fact.

The role of home environment in alcoholism was dramatically demonstrated back in the 1940s by Dr. Anne Roe of Harvard, who studied thirty-six children of alcoholic parents who had been reared apart from them. Roe examined them when they were in their 30s and found that none had any difficulty with alcohol. From this, Roe inferred that alcoholism is probably not inherited, and that its more common occurrence in children raised by alcoholic parents was brought on by the unfavorable environment.

Needless to say, these studies, along with those concluding exactly the opposite by finding a high incidence of alcoholism among the natural children of alcoholics raised in foster homes, can confuse the issue. It seems to make more sense to accept that a number of factors are at work in the development of problem drinking, and possibly more so in women, and that if genetic elements are involved they have to do with a tendency, a weakness, rather than an actual code for alcoholism stamped into the genes. This tendency may then be activated by an environmental influence. Seen in this light, the role of heredity becomes not deterministic but part of a spectrum of activities. It is reasonable to assume, then, that the woman who drinks is doing so for some reasons of which she is fully aware as well as for some of which she is totally unaware.

There is little doubt, for example, that sociocultural reasons are solidly behind the relatively high incidence of problem drinking among Indians as well as being important factors in the drinking behavior of women and Spanish-speaking and black Americans. In fact, much of the current literature seeking to explain drinking behavior and its causes among these groups focuses on sociocultural factors. Indians are plagued by higher rates of unemployment, low income, and poor education, all of which when combined result in unrealized goals that, in turn, can set people on the road to alcohol addiction. However, according to the NIAAA, these cultural explanations are varied and contradictory. They range from claims that moderate drunkenness is a substitute for lost traditions to the assertion that it relieves the anxieties and frustrations caused by the competition between the desire to yield to tradition and the pressure to integrate with the dominant culture.

The situation of the Cherokee woman underlines the special problems faced by Indians. In a survey of social problems among these women, Dr. Laurence French of the Western Carolina University Department of Sociology and Anthropology suggested that the Cherokee female is the one most affected by life on the reservation. More restricted than the Cherokee male, she carries the more lasting stigma of unacceptable social behavior through her role as biological mother and major socializing agent. But unlike other minority females caught in similar situations, Cherokee women retain a strong sense of individual freedom, and most will simply leave what they consider to be intolerable domestic situations, be it a burdensome mate or children.

Most Cherokee live below the poverty level—their average income is less than $3,000 a year for a family of four—and women head a large percentage of the total households. Not only is a woman in this situation, like the male, limited to the physical confines of the reservation, but she also suffers the "disgrace" of being a socially dependent female. Her ultimate dependency on federal and state agencies for her subsistence and her children's, along with her separation from and denial of the traditionally conservative life-style around her, leaves her extremely vulnerable to mental illness and alcoholism.

There is also the matter of learning in alcoholism. A woman might find, for example, that drinking will reduce fear and conflict and bring her some degree of pleasure. She drinks, feels good, and then stops. But then she discovers that she is fearful and miserable when she is sober. She drinks again, maybe more this time, and the addiction cycle is begun. It makes no real difference whether the source of tension is in the mind or in the body, according to the learning theory of alcoholism. The drinker drinks to feel pleasure or to avoid pain—it is a sort of conditioned reflex that is learned in a social setting where a particular kind of drinking behavior is prevalent.

One of those social settings—and a primary educator of drinking behavior—is the cocktail party, an institution as American as apple pie. We all have learned, either through experience or observation (Hollywood has recorded many), just what is "done" at a cocktail party: People mill about, glass in hand, for no purpose other than to exchange pleasantries and to drink. Since the pleasantries exchanged are generally trivial, more liquor than wisdom is absorbed. Such an opportunity to gather with friends in a cheerful atmosphere (made even more so with liquor) can be fun, so some people repeat the pattern in order to continue experiencing good times.

For those who drink to avoid pain, the cocktail party is a natural haven: Liquor abounds, so there's enough alcohol to block out almost anything; talk is superficial, so there's no worry that what you say will be upsetting to anyone, misconstrued, repeated, or even remembered. Dr. Morris Chafetz has characterized the unique American cocktail party better than anyone we know outside of T. S. Eliot:

"The cocktail party is supreme in emphasizing man's emotional isolation from man; his isolation from what he does, thinks, and feels. People are brought together, many of them unknown to one another, to drink, to talk, to be gay. The drinking is done under circumstances that engender little of the pleasurable responses of relaxation and socialization that alcohol can provide.

"The talk of the cocktail party emphasizes this. People do not listen, they do not care. All of us are familiar with the habitué of the cocktail party who, while pouring liquor into himself, pours into our ears the intimate details of his life he would never utter to a close friend. The reason for this is fairly obvious—we do not matter, we probably do not care. It is simpler to share intimate details of one's life with an individual with whom we are not emotionally involved than with those with whom we wish to continue our involvement. Words spoken at cocktail parties are often spoken to oneself rather than to another because excessive drinking creates a pharmacological barrier to emotional and social communication.

"Some people even think their heavy alcohol use encourages communication. But drinking that points in the direction of isolation, even in the midst of a crowd of persons, produces a liquor syndrome for perpetuating and intensifying alcohol problems."[10]

There is also evidence that many women now learn their drinking habit during adolescence. It has been suggested, too, that since girls reach puberty at an earlier age than they did fifty years ago, the physical and psychological difficulties brought about by this earlier onset, often aggravated by disintegrated family life, may be factors in their resorting to such socially acceptable drugs as alcohol and tobacco. One Boston-area study of college students found that the large majority of both women and men start to drink before college. In fact, their drinking in high school is the strongest indication of how much they will drink in college.

Dr. Graham B. Blaine, Jr., who has been chief of psychiatry at the Harvard University Health Services, once divided youthful drug-takers into three broad categories: the experience seeker, the oblivion seeker, and the personality change seeker. He then subdivided these into those who are influenced by more specific secondary motives. Thus, high school students take drugs usually to prove their courage, defy authority, attempt to increase sexual desire or performance, obtain a thrill, or find the meaning of life. College-age youths, Blaine said, take drugs more frequently in order to have the experience, reinforce their decision to drop out, communicate better, show up the "irrationality" of drug laws, and find a cure for emotional hangups. While Dr. Blaine did not address the issue of alcoholism, it would seem that a good deal of what he says can be applied to youthful drinkers of both sexes.

Many experience seekers, for instance, are motivated by rebellion. Because of real or fancied rejection by parents, they have stored up hostility, of which they may not be aware but which may be expressed by breaking rules. "This defiance," says Blaine, "is gratifying because it upsets their elders and brings attention from them. An angry parent may not be as enjoyable as a loving one, but he is more satisfying than a totally unresponsive one. An additional and more self-defeating satisfaction derived from being caught breaking the law is the retaliative pleasure gained from bringing disgrace to the family name and this constitutes a frequent unconscious motive for involvement with drugs."[11]

Rachel is 26 years old, an advertising copywriter in Boston, bright, articulate, and a regular drinker who worries about it:

My parents were very, very liberal in raising us but they had strict rules, too. My parents didn't drink very much, maybe a cocktail at night, but I never saw them drunk.

I had some trouble with drugs that started, I suppose, after I got rebellious. And after my father died, my mother was a lot more lenient. There were seven of us, and . . . she just kinda . . . turned her head. The other kids, who are older, were also into drugs and it might have been a case of my trying to be with them, getting them to accept me and so forth.

My family was very loving and demonstrative, we could talk about a lot of things, and we were, really, close-knit. The first time I smoked pot I was 12. I had visited my brother at Brown and everybody in the dorm was smoking, so I did, too. But you know, everybody was flipping out in those days. . . .

I remember a bad time. . . . I was going to New York City and I was seventeen, and it was during a really bad storm. We had had a long winter weekend at my school, and I went with one of my teachers and another student. At the airport, the plane was delayed for an hour because of the weather, so we went to the bar and we drank vodka gimlets. And I went into the bathroom and took about four Valiums. . . . my whole school was into alcohol and pills, that was the thing to do, we weren't any six-pack-of-beer-on-weekends-crowd. . . . And I came back to the bar and drank some more, another gimlet. Later, they snuck me into the men's room to smoke some grass. . . .

That combination, Valium and alcohol, was something I liked to do a lot. And I didn't even know it was that dangerous, can you believe it? It gave me a big boost . . . it was the best thing I had found of all the things I had tried. It felt the best to me. And I didn't know it was dangerous. I got into it in junior high school. Then the Karen Ann Quinlan thing happened, and it scared the hell out of me, that I had done something so dangerous. . . .

You know, I did everything you weren't supposed to do. . . . I did Valiums ten to twenty times, and I'd get it by lying about myself a lot to doctors. I'd call them and make up stories. A woman goes to a doctor, though, and it's easy. She's nervous, she says, and she's going to get Valium, no question about it. I also had a prescription I could refill, of fifty, and I could do that five times if I wanted. I also sold it.

I stopped taking Valium because I discovered speed and that was a lot nicer. I'd mix it with alcohol, and that's kind of neat because your head is . . . asleep, and your body is awake. You know what I mean? You can do things you can't do when you're drunk. Like dance all night. With Valium and alcohol, you're most likely to pass out. Later I did Quaaludes and alcohol, but only a couple of times because I knew that that was very dangerous. Those times, I remember, I could see everything but I couldn't react. It's like looking through a fish bowl, everything [is] so distorted and you feel like you can't do anything. . . .

It wasn't like I did it every day. I don't want to give that impression. Just on weekends.

During this time, I was very serious about school, and I never screwed up my grades. I was the valedictorian of my class. I guess it was a release. One of the reasons I didn't do it all that often was that I wasn't really bad. I was quite shy in high school, and I still am, I think. I never really belonged to a group, I had friends in every group. And that, maybe, was because we had done a lot of moving. I'd been to junior and senior high school in Providence, in Hartford, in Concord, New Hampshire. The dope and the liquor, I think, made people admire me. Now that I look back at it, I don't think a lot of the people in the groups in those different schools would do some of the things I would do. I was more daring and I think that 16- and 17-year-olds respected that. It gave me a place. I used to drink a lot and the boys used to really admire me. I could be one of them because I could do it all like they could. . . . I used to drink Jack Daniels straight out of the bottle and they never knew any girl who could do that. For some reason, at that time, it was important to me. . . .

Over the last couple of years, I had slacked off. I'd have a couple of drinks a couple of nights a week. But this year, it's been a little different. I have been drinking more and I'm more conscious of that fact. I don't usually drink by myself at home, unless I've had a tense day at work, and that's been happening a lot lately, too.

If I'm with a date, I drink a lot more. I see one guy right now [and] I'm with him almost every night, and I might have three a night. I think, sometimes, that if I lived with him or someone else I'd drink less because we wouldn't go out so much, and I think sometimes that I'm a bad influence on him, that he drinks because I want to have it.

I think I definitely do have an addictive personality. I made that clear to myself, I think, with the Valium thing. I was addicted to it. And I was addicted to marijuana, too. In my first year of college, I smoked every day, three to four times a day. As I said, I sold it, too, and that was to support the habit for other things. I got addicted to speed one summer, which is very hard to get off of. . . . So I know that once I start something it's hard for me to stop. I always wonder if it's happening with alcohol.

This man that I see, we've talked about it. If he's alone, he doesn't drink, and when we're out he tries, though I know it sounds patronizing, to get me off of it. He'll say, "You don't really need another one, do you?" The other night, this crazy thing happened. I wanted a drink and so we went to this bar and it was late, after a movie, and it was closed. So we went to this other place where they knew us and it was closed too, so we knocked on the door to see if they'd let us in. But there was no answer. So we went around to the kitchen because we knew the cook and we asked him to let us in. But he wouldn't and we started to get a little bit

. . . pushy. Finally it dawned on me what we were doing. I turned to my friend and I said, "Hey, are we alcoholics or something, we got to have a drink?" He said, "Yeah, it's pretty pathetic, isn't it?"

I think that in general I have a terrible problem with self-esteem. It's interesting, but in almost all of the things I've accomplished in my life I've had a man pushing me . . . teachers, bosses, the guy who tells me to stop drinking. They all tell me, look, you've got all this going for you, why don't you stop being so insecure about it and just do it. . . . It's not that easy.

PHYSIOLOGICAL CAUSES

Premenstrual tension and menopause have been implicated in female problem drinking by some researchers, but one cannot generalize about this. Suffice it to say that in some women hormone insufficiency can trigger a whole range of psychiatric symptoms, including psychotic depression and personality changes that can emotionally cripple a woman. In an attempt to alleviate the situation, women might turn to alcohol and other drugs, thus compounding their problem. If certain environmental factors also come into play, the situation could be further worsened, and problem drinking could well become a way of life.

This idea that some biological trigger touches off a craving for alcohol is an old one that has been extended to women via their endocrine systems. Studies have shown that drinking females register a significantly higher blood alcohol level during the premenstrual phase of their cycles than at any other time, leading to the supposition that there is an association between premenstrual tension and female intoxication and problem drinking. One study has, indeed, demonstrated that a group of alcoholic women related their drinking habits to their menstrual cycles.

Nearly thirty years ago, researcher Giorgie Lolli wrote: "Women are tied more than men to their biological selves.

Some biological phenomena such as menstruation . . . are events which affect women's behavior and which cast light on the close ties existing between women's physiology and their psychology. The link between these bioevents and excessive, uncontrolled drinking is clear-cut. For instance, it is frequently possible to see a connection between the onset of episodes of excessive and uncontrollable drinking and the onset of the menstrual period. . . . If the menopausal woman who is in the throes of depression bears within her those traits which are characteristic of addiction to alcohol, she might easily and quickly turn into a full-fledged alcoholic. . . . The medical histories of alcoholic women usually reveal a high incidence of surgical operations performed on the uterus or ovaries. They show that artificial menopause is often linked with an addiction pattern of drinking. Excessive and uncontrolled drinking appears also after miscarriages or abortions or after menstrual disorders of unknown causes."[12]

But as is often the case in research studies, other groups have failed to make the connection. It is doubtful that the menstrual cycle and premenstrual tension—which can unquestionably influence the way women handle alcohol—can alone be blamed for alcoholism and problem drinking. If that were the case, or if the rise and fall of hormone levels were somehow related directly to a craving for alcohol, as in the vitamin B theory, then the ranks of problem drinking would be infinitely larger than they are.

SOCIAL AND CULTURAL FORCES

Has the expansion of women's roles into areas that have been traditionally male had a measurable effect on alcohol-related problems among women? This central question is most difficult, and, in truth, there is no satisfactory answer. On one hand, there are those who argue that women's liberation has made drinking for women more acceptable, that there are more opportunities nowadays for women to drink, and, as we have seen, that job stress—both work pressure and anxiety caused by the still formidable barriers to promotion—and pressure from colleagues are important contributing factors. A former director of the National Institute of Alcohol Abuse and Alcoholism (NIAAA), has suggested that heavy drinking may result from dissatisfaction or confusion about self-identity brought on by a new consciousness and pressure for change. "Just as youth drink to achieve a demonstrable measure of adulthood, it may be that women who are confused about their current role are drinking heavily as a measure to indicate they have achieved equal status with men." It is true, for instance, that women between the ages of 25 and 44, when the impact of role shifts is felt most, are the most frequent users of psychiatric services.

Fifty years ago, Margaret Culkin Banning asked the question, "Why are so many women drinking now who were brought up in an atmosphere of strict temperance and whose very drinking tradition is against it?" Her answer might have been written today: "According to common testimony, many of them are drinking for social reasons. A cause frequently alleged is that because their friends drink, the habit is inescapable. It runs through groups, in circles, of which the beginning is hard to find. A second reason why they are drinking is because they have discovered that to do so gives them new sensations, fresh interests in old surroundings, and revives tired emotions. And a third reason, which is rarely given but which does often seem to underlie the others, is an almost feminist one. There are women who vaguely believe that drinking will open new doors to frankness and freedom, that in doing so they throw another unfair restraint on women into the discard and force men to share another privilege. In the defense they put up for their habits this belief bolsters them up. Many women are coming to believe and demand that the release (that drinking gives one), such as it is, should be theirs as well as men's. That is one of the underlying causes why women drink. I am not sure that the other causes do not possibly spring from it. Women do not see why men should have this stimulus to themselves, this pleasure, temporary or false though it may be. If it is one of the things men have kept to themselves for generations, women are curious to try it out. . . . What we are facing today is a resolve in women to look at life from every possible angle."[13]

Because of the current emphasis on women's upward mobility and the animosity this still touches off in a certain segment of the population, it has been easy for some to hold women's liberation accountable for aberrant drinking behavior. However, others argue that this is both ridiculous and unfair. Says Edith Gomberg: "There is, in fact, a lot of disagreement as to whether the emancipation of women lessens or magnifies the extent of alcoholism among them. I don't see how such a question can be really resolved—it is an emotional issue, complexly tying women's rights, changes in patterns of acceptable social behavior, the dissatisfactions and frustrations of contemporary existence—and alcohol. But we would be foolish to accept a simple formula. To say, 'Free women from Kuche, Kirche, Kinder* and end alcoholism' is as silly as saying the emancipation of women leads to alcoholism and moral decay."

It has also been suggested that while factors spawned by the women's movement could cause some women to drink more, emancipation might have some positive effects with regard to women and alcohol. "To the extent that it can free both men and women from rigid notions about proper male and female behavior and help them accept and actualize their own unique blends of assertiveness, nurturance, achievement and sensitivity, it may help reduce drinking problems by decreasing the types of sex-role conflicts which cause problems for many of today's alcoholic women," says Dr. Wilsnack.

* Kitchen, Church, Children

Age, marital status, ethnic background, employment and
socioeconomic status—all of these may also play a part in the
development of a drinking problem in women. Although no
accurate portrait of the background of a woman who abuses alcohol can be drawn, there are some rough profiles of the
women arrested for DWI, among them this one constructed by
the Boston researchers who studied arrest patterns: "Quite
generally, she is a woman in her early 30s who is legally unattached and living alone. She has a job of relatively low-level
skill, when employed, despite a slightly higher than average
level of education. She is usually arrested during late-evening
and early-morning hours as a result of a traffic violation, involvement in an automobile accident, or abusive behavior. She
is usually alone in the car and highly intoxicated. This high
level of intoxication is symptomatic of an alcohol problem
which is reflected in a high rate of divorce–separation and previous involvement with the police and courts. Their social characteristics and circumstances of arrest appear to depict a group
of isolated individuals seeking solutions or relief via the mechanism of local drinking establishments."

One thing to remember when considering social background and its role in female problem drinking is that the
studies rely, as do all such surveys, on lower-, middle-, or
upper-middle-class women. It's been suggested that the classic
profile—later abuse of alcohol than men, drinking alone and
because of a stressful event—is not a definitive one because it
fits only the higher-status woman. The lower socioeconomic
group of women is more likely to begin getting into trouble
with liquor at an earlier age; to drink visibly and in situations or
places, such as in a men's bar, that other women would avoid;
and to get into more difficulty, both with the law and with
others, because of the drinking. The skid-row woman is a case
in point. In the first place, she generally differs from skid-row
men in that she is more inclined to cite a failed marriage as the

reason for her hitting the bottom, or is more likely to come from a broken home. She also differs from high-status problem-drinking women in her inability to hide her drinking, in the earlier onset of drinking, and in her bender-style of drinking.

With regard to marital status, the NIAAA points out that among women under 35, there is little difference in drinking habits between single and married women, but divorced and separated women have the highest incidence of heavier and problem drinking of any group. However, where comparisons are possible, the older women who are divorced, separated, and widowed show lower problem rates than those who are married. Since the divorced status is likely to be more recent for the younger woman than for the older one, it has been suggested that the crisis of divorce or separation, rather than the status of being divorced, is responsible for the increased rates of heavier and problem drinking for younger women.

The NIAAA also reports that among married women under 65, those who are working have higher rates of heavier and problem drinking than those who are not employed outside the home, regardless of socioeconomic status. "This finding may stem from peer pressures in the working situation to drink more frequently," says a government report, "accompanied by few inner constraints not to do so. An alternative explanation associates elevated rates with conflicts stemming from the dual demands of the roles of wife and employee."

In connection with this role conflict, one study cited by the NIAAA made use of a sex-role index that classified women 30 to 64 years of age into "in role" and "out of role" groups. To be out of role, women who drink are more often heavy drinkers and problem drinkers, regardless of socioeconomic status. This demonstrates, once again, the very special circumstances and stresses that play a key part in why women drink. It would seem that women who know their place, and who do not agonize over

it, so to speak, who do not range too far beyond the confines of
their sex, are "rewarded" with fewer problems with alcohol
than their sisters who break out.

This holds true, also, for lesbians, a minority group often
maligned, misunderstood, and discriminated against. They are
women who know full well the meaning of despair, low self-
image, and alienation, and many of them learn quickly that alcohol can brighten their world temporarily. For those who
choose such an outlet—and there is little reliable data on lesbians who do or do not drink or on how the drinkers might differ from non-gay women drinkers—there are the parties and
gay bars, where, according to one study in Los Angeles, the
regulars spend an average of 80 percent of their time. The lesbian problem drinker has an especially difficult time of it for
she is faced with the choice of either going to the gay bar and
not drinking, or avoiding the bar entirely. The first is tough
enough for anyone with a drinking problem, the second means
shunning an important cultural support system.

Sadder still is that the current alcoholism treatment facilities do not deal adequately with lesbian drinkers. Says one
counselor: "In many alcoholism programs, women feel they
have to hide their lesbianism, pass for straight, and act un-
natural when their lovers come to visit. In halfway houses, they
are sometimes prevented from seeing their lesbian friends
while there. There is also an assumed cause-effect relationship
between drinking and lesbianism that is expressed two ways.
People think she is a lesbian because she got drunk and went
wrong. She is told that if she stops drinking, everything will get
right and she will go straight. Or, people think she's a lesbian
and therefore sick, so she gets drunk. Solve the lesbianism, and
she'll surely stop drinking. This may be confusing for her. She
may be happy being gay, but she still wants to stop drinking."

Women alcoholics, then, are a heterogeneous group.
They sometimes drink for the same reasons that men do, and

they often have, as do men, an alcoholic parent. But their reasons for drinking can also often differ from men's, and even from other women's. Beyond that—beyond the drinking patterns and the reasons behind them, beyond the theories and the suggestions and the studies—there is one truth: the reality that the woman with an alcohol problem is not an anomaly among drinkers. She may have deviated from society's rules, both medical and social, and she may have her own gender-inspired reasons for doing so, but she is not alone in her disorder and in the personal inadequacy that may be at the root of it. She has a lot of company, both men and women, and she is, in that sharing, more an equal than she was in the traditional American role that society expected of her and which may have driven her to drink. It is a painful rite of passage but it may, with its message that alcoholism is not a man's illness, help topple some of the barriers of harsh judgment that have been erected not only in the path of acceptance and treatment of the woman drinker, but also in the way of equality of the sexes in all other things.

3

The Woman
ALCOHOLIC

When I'm alone, I might open a bottle of wine if I've had a bad day. I'll read and be drinking this wine, and the thing that frightens me is that after I've had one glass I don't want to get up, so I'll drink the whole bottle, maybe til I'm good and drunk. And I have to admit I've even done that on nights when I wasn't depressed.

What worries me is that I don't think I'm going to know I'm in any kind of real trouble with this alcohol until I'm really in trouble. I think there's a real fine line between being an alcoholic and . . . the sort of drinker I am. I worry sometimes that I'm going to wake up some morning and realize I'm a drunk.

Tina, a 28-year-old credit manager

Alcoholism has been described as one part physical, one part psychological, one part sociological, and one part alcohol. The description is apt and should make one pause before suggesting that the woman who drinks too much does so for this or that reason. To implicate one causative factor as the prime culprit is as ridiculous as saying flatly that brain chemicals are the sole cause of mental illness.

There is no lack of theories to explain why men drink, why women drink, why people in general drink. In the previous chapter we read of the alcoholic, or addictive, personality; of alcoholics who drink to escape from tensions or frustrations; of alcoholism as an inherited trait; of irresponsible drinking behavior being learned from parents or peers; of biochemical defects that force one to use alcohol improperly; of allergic reactions; of weak-willed individuals who cannot withstand seduction by liquor; of vitamin deficiencies and even glandular abnormalities as causes.

Any of these "causes" may well be implicated at one time or another in alcoholism. But, again, no one factor can be singled out. Remember that not everyone who drinks has a problem handling alcohol, that liquor affects different people in very different ways, and that some of the traits ascribed to alcoholics are often found in women and men who are not alcoholic but who are mentally ill—or who are normal. There is also the very difficult task of defining such terms as alcoholism, alcohol-related disability, excessive drinking, problem drinking, and social drinking. Sometimes the line between alcoholism and problem drinking is blurred and, indeed, it may be argued that there is no difference at all.

It is important to know, however, that merely tallying the glasses or bottles drunk by a woman or a group is no real measure of whether or not someone has a drinking problem. There are any number of people, even whole societies, who consume enormous quantities of alcoholic beverages yet do not classify as alcoholic. On the other hand, the Swedes, who have one of the lowest rates of consumption, have one of the highest incidences of alcoholism. Heavy daily drinking may well imply an abnormal pattern, and it may indeed lead to physical and psychological dependency on alcohol, but one cannot assume that this will happen. What, then, is this disorder we know as alcoholism?

The words of one counselor in a women's treatment center sums it up fairly accurately: "First the woman takes a drink, then the drink takes a drink, and finally, the drink takes the woman." The key word in any definition of alcoholism is addiction—which, incidentally, ought not to be confused with habit, as it so often is. If, for example, you are a habit smoker, or you have formed the habit of drinking coffee, you are not addicted in the true sense. You may stop smoking or drinking coffee and although you'll undoubtedly crave what you've given up, even grow tense, you won't react in the way you would if you were an alcoholic and you quit drinking.

An alcoholic is physically addicted, or dependent, which means that she or he may experience severe withdrawal symptoms hours after drinking is stopped. These can include headache, nausea, mental confusion, cramps, vomiting, tremors, all of which may be alleviated by resumption of drinking, a fact the alcoholic realizes. Alcoholics are also psychologically addicted to the drug—that is, they have a compulsive need for liquor to lift an emotional burden. They may not even like the taste, and drink only to escape or to bolster their concept of self. Everyone is psychologically dependent on something to some extent: on television, possibly; on certain foods; on money, or dancing, or people. Even moderate drinkers who have no difficulty with liquor often, as we all know, enjoy a drink to relax, either occasionally or regularly.

It is only when the dependency becomes strong, when drinking becomes a psychological escape hatch every time a crisis occurs, when the dependency harms the individual or others around her, that there is something to worry about. At that point we are talking again about compulsion, that irresistible urge to drink alcohol on a continuous or periodic basis. The American Medical Association has defined alcoholism as "an illness characterized by preoccupation with alcohol and loss of control over its consumption, such as to lead usually to intoxication if drinking; by chronicity; by progression; and by a tendency toward relapse. It is typically associated with physical disability and impaired emotional, occupational and/or social adjustments as a direct consequence of persistent excessive use. . . . In short, alcoholism is regarded as a type of drug dependence of pathological extent and pattern, which ordinarily interferes seriously with the patient's total health and adaptation to environment."

Alcoholics have been described as those who are consistently unable to choose whether they will drink or not and, if they do drink, are consistently unable to choose whether they will stop or not. Another description is those who drink alcohol to the point that it interferes with some or all of the everyday aspects of life. The World Health Organization has also described the addiction, taking note of the various types of alcoholism, which differ from culture to culture: "A chronic, behavioral disorder, marked by repeated drinking of alcohol in excess of the dietary and social customs of the community and to an extent that it interferes with the drinker's health or how he functions socially or economically."

This brings up the matter of how alcoholism is classified. In the Ninth Revision of the International Classification of Diseases, it is termed alcohol dependence syndrome, but its inclusion in the standard compilation gives it standing as a disease, which is generally defined as "a disturbance in the structure or function of an organ or organs." It is not our purpose to enter into a semantic discussion of the differences, if any, between disease, disorder, illness, and sickness. There are some health professionals who, along with Alcoholics Anonymous, insist that the term "disease" is an appropriate one, because alcoholism has a cause or causes, symptoms, unhealthy effects on mind and body, and prescribed treatment. On the other hand, many feel that "disease" is a misnomer; that it implies an illness involving specific agents of infection, like bacteria or viruses; and that the label misleads one into believing that a cure is now or may one day be possible. "The truth is," says David Davies, "that the disease concept of alcoholism is a red herring. How far it is true at all is a separate question. . . . The concept is usually invoked to elicit sympathy for alcoholics, to alter society's treatment of them, and to query their responsibility in law for some of their acts. It has no bearing at all in the framing of a definition, satisfactory for everyday working purposes and heuristically valuable. Indeed, in the absence of such a definition, no one will ever be able to say whether alcoholism is a disease or not, but that is the very least merit claimed for the definition proposed here. . . . Alcoholism is intermittent or continual use of alcohol associated with dependency (psychological or physical) or harm in the sphere of mental, physical, or social activity. This definition, it is submitted, is economical and simple. It provides an essential framework into which to fit the problem, and allows us to go ahead with fact finding to ascertain the truth (as distinct from the legends which surround the subject)."[1]

We would agree. Moreover, we would add that while there is no question that the alcoholic is disabled, addition of the "ism" to the name implies a doctrine, or system. And there is, in the final analysis, no such structure, for what is called alcoholism has no well-defined symptoms, shared by all troubled by it; no proven cause; no single treatment. To call it a disease, as we would call diabetes or polio or measles, is to ignore the complexity of a multifaceted behavioral condition, a preoccupation with alcohol that is a drastic response to a mix of psychological, sociological, and biological events.

One has to remember that alcoholism is associated with both the effects of alcohol on the drinker, and those factors *within* the drinker that lead her or him to misuse it. About the only thing we can say with any certainty is that alcohol affects drinkers in many different ways, and that the reasons each is so affected—along with the reasons each misuses alcohol—do not lend themselves easily to categorizing. Women differ from one another in how alcohol affects them and in why they drink. The same thing holds true for men. But it is also true that alcohol affects women in different ways than it affects men, and that women's drinking patterns and the reasons why they misuse alcohol differ from those of men. Trying to sort out all of these factors is no simple task, and the "disease" label is but a convenient out.

If alcoholism fails to convey the complexities of the issue, problem drinking is also a broad term. The National Institute of Alcohol Abuse and Alcoholism, which lists both alcoholism and problem drinking in its reports, defines a problem drinker as "a person who drinks alcohol to an extent or in a manner that an alcohol-related disability is manifested. Therefore, the term problem drinker generally is applied to those who demonstrate problems in relation to drinking alcohol." An alcohol-related disability exists when the physical, mental or social functioning of an individual is impaired, and there is reasonable evidence that alcohol is part of the cause of that disability. Impairment includes health problems related to specific drinking patterns; offensive behavior caused by heavy drinking; injuries, death, or property loss caused by accidents associated with drinking; failure of the chronic excessive drinker to live up to the responsibilities of home or job; and emotional problems that are linked to drinking. An alcohol-related disability, like problem drinking, does not require the presence of addiction, the loss of self-control, that is characteristic of the so-called alcoholic.

But probably the best way to define problem drinking is drinking enough and in such a way to cause trouble for oneself or for society. Remember that a common factor in all drinking problems—excessive drinking, alcohol-related disabilities, problem drinking, and what is called alcoholism—is the negative effect on both the drinker and her associates.

Thus far, we have been discussing some of the definitions

of alcoholism and problem drinking for both sexes. But no matter how one labels the dependency, women who drink excessively usually have some specific drinking practices. And, although we can again point to no woman as a typical problem drinker, we can highlight those habits that research has identified as common to many female alcoholics.

• Women drink, on the average, less amounts than men, and they prefer liquor and wine to beer. Advertising may play a significant role here, with its generally male bias toward beer and ale, and its presentation of the sophisticated, cocktail-drinking woman. During teen years, beer is the beverage of choice among both men and women, although some surveys have suggested that even teenaged women tend to drink hard liquor more often than young men.

• Women do not buy as many drinks as men, probably because men often maintain the tradition of picking up the check. Also, society still does not condone drunkenness in women, so women, aware of this, may consciously keep their public intake down, which might correspond to their buying fewer drinks.

• Women who drink a lot generally begin doing so at a later age than men, usually in their 30s (as opposed to men's 20s), but once they start, their drinking problems develop faster, and they appear to enter treatment at the same age as men, around 45. The NIAAA points out that among women there is a higher incidence of heavier and problem drinkers in the 35-to-64 age group than in either the younger or older groups. The sole exception seems to occur for divorced and separated women in the under-35 category. Says Harvard's Dr. Sharon Wilsnack: "Women are different and this difference (earlier age of onset of excessive drinking) probably relates to the different social norms about drinking for men and women. Drinking is much more tied up with the traditional male role (for example, the idea of 'drinking like a man'), and for this reason alcohol may hold an attraction and a mystique for men that it doesn't for most women. . . . Although the more rapid development of

alcoholism in women is sometimes said to be evidence that
women alcoholics are 'sicker' or more 'pathological' than men
alcoholics, it seems just as likely that the rapid development of
women's alcohol problems reflects the more punitive social
reaction to problem drinking in women, which tends to accelerate the vicious cycle of drinking: social disapproval and
rejection—more drinking."[2]

•   Middle-aged women drink alone more often than men,
drink more often at home with family and less frequently in
single-sex groups, public places, or private clubs. College-age
women, on the other hand, report drinking primarily in small
groups of mixed sexes or with one person of the opposite sex.
Again, social sanctions may play a bigger role here than a pref-
erence on the woman's part for seclusion.

•   Many married women often tend to drink heavily on
weekends or at parties, and not as frequently throughout the
week.

•   Alcoholic women are far more likely to drink with a husband or a male companion than alcoholic men are to drink with
wife or a woman friend.

•   Because of the social stigma attached to a woman with a
drinking problem, she is more apt to manipulate her environment to suit or cover up her drinking. As Sandra says,

I used to do things like adopt a new identity so I could drink. You
know, the con art of the alcoholic is to get other people to help you drink
without your having to ask. Like one time, this guy asked me out, and he
was really nice. So, I got myself all dressed up in jeans and a jersey, but the
thing is that's not me at all, jeans and jersey. But I knew he was the sort of
guy who liked to go to jazz places dressed down and I knew that he'd be
going there, and I didn't like jazz at all. So, the jeans I put on made me
feel like a new person, a different person, and when I started drinking,
as I knew I would that night, it wouldn't really be me who was doing it,
but the other person, the woman in jeans and jersey. It was my cover-up.
And I used to walk into a package store every so often, and I'd play the
poor dumb girl act, tell the man I was having a party and ask him what

do guys like to drink, what's the strongest proof gin and vodka, all that. I'd call up guys I knew drank, I'd walk into a bar alone pretending I was looking for someone and looking forlorn until someone bought me a round, I'd borrow rum from the neighbors to make what I told them was my favorite cake, I'd volunteer to make the punch at parties, I'd do all those things that didn't make me like myself very much anymore. One time, on my birthday, I made it a point to tell everyone about it so they'd all buy me a round.

The only person who saw through it, though, was my mother. She was one smart lady. She'd say she could always tell when I was manipulating things to go off on a binge because I'd call her on the phone, that was a form of manipulation. I'd call her and I'd be all lovely and gushy, and I suppose it was my way of telling her I was a good person, and was sort of looking for sympathy and comfort before I let go because I knew that I wasn't going to be a very good person when I started the booze.

• Women who drink obsessively show up less often for treatment than men. It was true for some time that for every woman who sought help for problem drinking, there were at least five men. This was so for two reasons: First, women were protected from "going public" by friends and relatives who disguised the problem with a less embarrassing diagnosis. Second, alcoholic treatment programs were ill-equipped to deal with females. Today, however, more women are entering treatment, more women are openly admitting their problem, and their families and friends are also less reluctant. Also, women are more likely than men to report that their drinking is out of control and, when they do show up for treatment, to be more realistic than men about the problem. Thus, say some specialists, the prognosis for treatment should be more favorable for women than men. However, other studies point out that once a woman is in treatment, she often doesn't do as well as men, has longer hospitalizations and lower success rates. Says Wilsnack: "The more limited success of women alcoholics in treatment is sometimes interpreted as further evidence that alcoholic women are 'sicker' than their male counterparts. However, it seems equally plausible that the low success rates are due primarily to our failure to develop treatment programs which are sensitive to the special problems and special needs of alcoholic women."

•   Some studies have suggested that more women than men drink when tense, to celebrate or to cheer themselves up; that is, they are more inclined to credit drinking with psychosocial benefits. According to these studies, women are more likely to regard alcohol as a medicinal agent—a view that, as one specialist has suggested, may be an expression of a woman's need to rationalize her drinking in this manner. Men, on the other hand, are supposedly more likely to drink to meet women, to get drunk, or to loosen up.

They call her Arabian Mary because of her nose, which is like the one Anthony Quinn had in *Lawrence of Arabia*. She is 39 and a heavy drinker:

Quite honestly, I don't feel the guilt so much when I'm drinking. All I know is it does make me feel good, forget things that bother me. I get along better with people. I see men, different ones, so I'm not one of those people who's depressed and alone a lot.

I truly enjoy drinking, I really do, and I suppose that's why I haven't ever really gone for help. I'm not really sure how serious the problem is. I know I need liquor, I like it, the taste and the effect, and I can put away quite a lot in a night. I don't count, do you?

No, I don't keep it in my desk and belt it down in the lady's room during coffee break. That's movie stuff. It's never really ever interfered with my doing my job, and I don't drink in the morning, although that's never bothered me when I hear people do it; after all, the sun's gone down over the yardarm somewhere on this earth. . . .

I'm out every night after work with the crowd from the office, and I don't drink alone at home like the typical woman you read about in Redbook. *I would, I suppose, if I didn't have anybody to go with, and that's not the case. I do like the conviviality of it all. The thing is, I can't really enjoy an evening out without a drink, can you?*

Sometimes I do sort of panic out on those few occasions when I've been invited and there's no liquor. When that happens, I just leave early and go somewhere where I know I'll find friends. There's no kick in being with people who're just into Virgin Marys. I think you have to be able to get a little glow on, a buzz. My God, that's life, isn't it?

Most of the crowd I hang with is a drinking crowd, and so we don't have anyone who talks about the virtues of being a teetotaler. That's no fun. No, I've never denied I drink a lot. But does that have to be a problem? According to the shrinks, if you have to have it, it's a problem. Well, I have to have food and sleep and sex, too, and those aren't problems, are they?

•   The steady-drinking woman is less likely to delude herself into believing that she can stop when she chooses. Men, on the other hand, appear to be more hopeful about their ability to control their drinking. And steady-drinking women have more regimented drinking plans than do steady-drinking men.

•   Women may be less inclined than men to continue drinking heavily while employed.

•   Alcoholic women complain of general dissatisfaction with sexual contact, and appear to have a high incidence of partial, if not complete, inability to achieve orgasm. Sexual dysfunction, in fact, appears to be one of the most prevalent problems associated with women's drinking habits. One study of forty-four acknowledged women alcoholics conducted at the University of Utah Medical Center concluded that women alcoholics seem to want intimacy, but simultaneously avoid it because of past interpersonal experiences.

Among other findings in the Utah study were these:

1. Nearly 40 percent of the respondents said they had been raped at some time in their life. (Ten percent is considered a reasonable estimate for the general population.)

2. About 40 percent experienced incest, defined as "sexual activity with a relative." (Only about 5 percent of the general population has similar experiences.)

3. Fifty-five percent indicated they would like to receive sex therapy for their problems, and an additional 20 percent felt they might benefit from such help.

4. One-third reported feeling used during sexual activity.

5. The majority reported that they used alcohol prior to sexual activity, and most felt it helped them relate to members of the opposite sex.

6. Nearly 20 percent reported they had never experienced orgasm (more than double the number in the general population).

7. Thirty-six percent indicated they experienced orgasm less than 5 percent of the time.

8. Seventy-one percent said they had been involved in extramarital affairs, most of short duration.

9. Over 20 percent reported occasional homosexual experiences since adolescence.

•   Other research has suggested that along with sexual dissatisfaction, the alcoholic woman's marriage is often a nightmare. She frequently marries a man many years her senior with whom she is incompatible. Often he is also an alcoholic and physically abusive. Over 40 percent, one researcher found, suffer broken marriages.

This same researcher points out also that the notion that women who drink have loose morals is a myth. He found that the popular image of the scarlet woman is pure fiction: Only about 5 percent of all women drinkers could be termed promiscuous, and most of the remaining 95 percent reported a diminished interest in sex. The aphrodisiac powers of alcohol, he adds, are greatly magnified in the eyes of the public. There is scant evidence that sexual behavior exhibited while drinking is due solely to the powers of liquor. Promiscuity while drinking may instead be a reflection of a sexual proclivity that comes to the fore when societal inhibitions are diminished.

Again, all of the above are general statements that may not always hold true in each and every case. Also, one has to consider that times are changing; that the barriers separating the sexes are falling, albeit slowly; that the drinking patterns of women and men are beginning to coalesce; that the pejorative comments about women's drinking habits are lessening; that, indeed, problem drinking in women may not, in the last analysis, be all that different from that in men. The studies relating to drinking behavior that have been cited throughout this book are by no means exhaustive ones and we doubt that there are any such. Data gatherers often have a preconceived notion of their work, and it is no secret that while statistics may not necessarily lie, they will most certainly, as the late New York Mayor Fiorello LaGuardia once said, testify for either side.

As we have seen, no one can say with the utmost certainty that feelings of inadequacy and frustration over being unable to fulfill a woman's role and low self-esteem are causes by themselves of alcoholism or emotional disorder, but it is known that women with decreased self-image are more apt to misuse or abuse alcohol, behavior that in turn lowers self-esteem even more. In fact, the self-esteem of alcoholic women is often a good deal lower than that of male alcoholics and of non-alcoholic women. This has been demonstrated not only by data gathered from self-esteem questionnaires, but by a technique that has been used by psychologists for years to examine various personality aspects: free drawing. It is not unusual for a woman alcoholic to draw pictures of trees stripped of leaves, of human figures with dejected facial expressions, of herself as a small individual standing beside larger people, of herself in the role of a murderer's victim.

This feeling of "smallness" that plagues the alcoholic woman as well as many other women in our society has a great deal to do with the accepted role of woman as rescuer, as service-oriented. Groomed from the outset to do for others first, to put others ahead of herself, she develops the subservient tone that contributes to lowered self-esteem. A young suicidal woman put it this way: "Jesus is first, others are second, and I am third."

Because women have been so historically, psychologically, and economically dependent on men yet so conscious of men's needs, it is often impossible for them to break this tight bond and view themselves as independently functioning people. Let something go awry with a male-female relationship and it is the woman who is more apt to be filled with guilt, to feel blame and self-deprecation, and a sense of failure. In such a situation, some women will seek therapy. Others will turn to other outlets for consolation: They enter new relationships, which always carry the risk of increasing the guilt and self-hatred, or overindulge in alcohol, other drugs, even food. Many throw themselves into their work with a vengeance, becoming compulsive housecleaners, for example. "It is pretty safe to say," as one reformed woman alcoholic described it, "that we are all running from something."

Psychological stress takes many forms and women respond very individually to it. Because women, as a group, are only recently learning to like themselves, it will be some time before they can learn to actually love themselves. When that happens, when women learn to recognize who they are and the capacity of their resources, they will become responsible for themselves and dependent on others only enough to maintain the balance that is so essential.

Women often get pulled down by the notion that their problems are theirs alone and, until very recently, this is how most felt about the alcohol problem. But there is tremendous emphasis today on the need for women to come together and communicate because women understand women and the potential for self-discovery and growth is greater in groups. Personal connections are made; barriers of age, economics, worldly experiences, race, culture—all the barriers that in male or mixed society have always seemed so difficult to cross—are ignored. It is repeatedly recognized that groups work well.

In general, society values women according to the male definition. Perhaps the saddest women are those who rely totally on the status afforded them by their husband's profession. Women who don't get out of this bind of blind comfort set themselves up for false competition and low self-esteem.

It is a difficult road for women, and doubly so for the alcoholic woman. On one hand, she may want to take care of it all on her own; on the other, she fears she may be abandoned by friends and therapist if she falls from what she perceives as their estimation of her. Thus, she lapses, and begins to depend on others once again, not only for the comforting care they can give, but for her very sense of self-worth and identity. And in that course lies the pitfall of addiction.

Today's woman has more challenging options open to her, and though they are not always offered willingly, they are there. But the game, as they say, must often be played against the big guys. Her desire is to control her own life without giving up the values that she has been conditioned to believe are essential—indeed mandatory. She asks for divorce, deserts her role as wife and mother, and must suffer the heat that comes with her decision. But the risk must be taken. As writer Annie Gottlieb has said: "Exceptional women have always braved loneliness, disapproval, and danger to follow their stars; and genuine risks were intrinsic to women's traditional role, as the Aztecs recognized when they honored a woman in childbirth as the equal of a warrior in battle."[3]

Taking risks often means letting go—letting go to perhaps live life more fully, to enter into a concentrated search for your real self—and this almost always raises conflict. Conflict means decision-making, which leads to losses as well as gains. But if you are lucky, the gain side of the scale will mean growth and rewarding self-knowledge.

Recovered women alcoholics know about this: They have experienced it and witnessed it in others. Those who make it, although they believe in taking one day at a time and never feeling too sure that they have licked the habit, speak with a determination and courage that is to be envied.

Diana is 46 and black, a secretary in a San Francisco bank:

I know now, from going to AA meetings, that all the people I was with who bought me drinks all the time, my drinking, all that, I had absolutely no control over. It was the alcohol telling me who to go with, the addiction telling me what to do, how much to drink.

You learn you have a disease, and I believe that. There's nothing you can do about yesterday or tomorrow, so what you do is today. And if nobody wants to forgive me, then they'll have to live with that, just [as] I got to live with what I am. You have to be honest with yourself. . . . I have gone down as far as I could go.

Recovered alcoholics have walked among the dead, they have been to the other side, and they have been given another chance to return to this reality. And somehow this experience, terrible though it may be, leaves them stronger. These women are the real risk takers.

Ruby Folsom Austin, "Big Ruby," is 67, tall, colorful, and outspoken. The mother of Cornelia Wallace, former First Lady of Alabama, she is also the sister of Jim Folsom, former governor of Alabama. Her habit, for thirty-five years, was bourbon:

I was a Good Friday child, born on that day in 1913, my momma's best child, and I started sippin' at about 35, Champagne, social drinkin' and the weakness ran in the family—not the women, just the men. We had a lot of parties, and we used to get it by the case, it was given to us, he was the governor, my brother, and naturally the agencies gave it to him. . . . So, I'd hide it, and my Bible-totin' sister'd go through the house seein' what she could find. . . . My cousin hid my Champagne, gave it away, I don't know what he did with it, but anyway he said one time, "I'll pour you a little bourbon," and I said, "Well, put it in Coca-Cola," and pretty soon I was drinkin' it with water, and it just grew and I learned to like bourbon. . . .

Everybody knew I drank, but they respected it. They didn't want it in the paper and all that. I wasn't that kind of a drinker. I drank at parties. I was a social drinker for so long, oh yeah, for so long. It just caught up with me. . . .

But you know, my sister used my drinking as an excuse to fight me. She didn't want me around. If I had drunk as much whiskey as my sister said I drank, I'd 'a been dead twenty years ago. . . . I was just sippin'. . .

And you know, my daughter, she cut off all my calls and that wasn't nice. It made it worse, and I cried all the time because she was so . . . ugly to me. I was upset with her, too, and I was worse upset than she was.

I just love people, love to be with them. Grew up with a bunch of boys, had company all the time. Momma'd have three cooks on Sunday and we'd invite everybody we wanted to. . . . Politics indeed does call for a lot of drinkin', yes it does, I'd put a yes to that. I was born with it, and it was easy to do. I used to say I wasn't goin' to. I used to say to my brother, James, "You'll be the master of your soul or the bottle will be, you just make your mind up now, James." And I said, "If you quit that drinkin' and tend to your business and don't let that whiskey get to you like it got to some other Folsoms, you can be president of the United States with your looks and your personality and your political background." And he'd say, "Oh, no Southerner ever goin' to be president of the United States. . . ." You know, he quit drinkin' the last time he was governor, and he told me to stop, that I had to quit drinkin' so much. . . .

First time I tried treatment I think I lasted two weeks. I got back on. We had gone to dinner, picked up a floor show, and I slipped away to get a drink so wouldn't anybody know it. I tried to hide it for a while, but it didn't stay hid very long. . . .

Well, I made up my mind that I wanted to go for treatment, and I needed to go. I knew I was an alcoholic and I meant business. And when I mean business I stick to it. But, see, I hated to face the fact that I was an alcoholic, it's hard as hell to admit it. You tell yourself a million times you can quit it but you can't. I had come to the point where I could not stop on my own. I'd go two weeks. . . . But it isn't goin' to be that way again. I understand this thing, and it's either that or be six feet under and, brother, I'm havin' such a good time—I'm not ready to die.

I'm public now because I feel if it can help someone who's drinkin' then I'll do it. When I first decided to go public with it, why they all . . . thought [I'd] be so nervous on that radio talk show with Wilbur Mills, they thought I'd be so nervous Cornelia'd have to warm me up. I said, "Honey, ain't nobody ever had to warm Big Ruby up to talk, baby. I was born talkin'." My brother-in-law called me Polly 'cause I talked like a parrot. . . .

I'm not narrow-minded about drinkin' because people can do it, that's great—anybody can handle it, great. Don't you think? Anybody can drink social, more power to 'em. But I had ceased to drink that way.

Now I feel good, doin' a lot better, real proud, real glad. . . .[4]

4

The Effects
OF
ALCOHOL

*It was a time of nightmare; I had days of wondering whether I
had not already died and was in hell. There were days when I could
not open the blinds, nights when I dared not turn out the lights.*
A mother in AA

Consider, for a moment, your liver, your body's largest
glandular organ. Located in the upper right side of the abdom-
inal cavity, it is a complex chemical workshop associated with
dozens of functions of chemistry and metabolism. It produces
the bile that helps you digest fatty foods; it manufactures hepa-
rin, an anticoagulant; it stores and releases sugar. The liver also
produces antibodies that help ward off disease, cleanses the
body of poisons, and, most important in our consideration of
alcohol, produces enzymes that accelerate the thousands of
changes going on continually in our bodies. Without
enzymes—and there are more than 100,000 of these chemical

workhorses in every cell—your blood cells wouldn't be re-
plenished, your food would go undigested, your body wouldn't
build tissue.

Enzymes have a specific job to do. In fact, whenever a gene,
the unit responsible for heredity, wants something done it
makes a specific enzyme to get it done. There is, in fact, one enzyme responsible for the breakdown of alcohol. Called alcohol
dehydrogenase, or ADH, it is found chiefly in the liver. When
you drink moderate amounts of wine, beer, or liquor, the ADH
supply is able to handle them relatively well. It should be
pointed out here that alcohol is normally present in all mam-
mals, a category that, of course, includes humans. It is produced continually in the intestinal tract by micro-organisms
working on soluble sugars and, according to recent studies,
even the insides of a teetotaler may produce enough alcohol to
equal what you might get in a quart of 3.2 beer every day. This
naturally produced alcohol, however, does not reach the brain
because the ADH in the liver gets rid of it quickly, before it can
seep out into the circulatory system.

But when there is an overload of alcohol in the system,
ADH has to work double-time, and if the strain is constant the
result can be devastating—an inflammatory disease known as
cirrhosis. Occurring about eight times more often among alcoholics than in non-alcoholics, cirrhosis is characterized by the
replacement of liver cells with tough, fibrous scar tissue. In its
advanced stages, passage of blood through the now-hardened
liver is obstructed.

The symptoms, progression, and death rates associated
with the disease are similar in women and men, but there is an
interesting sidelight to the statistics that have been compiled
about the disease, one that relates directly to the drinking patterns of many women. For at least fifty years, the rates of cirrhosis among women have not increased as markedly as they
have among men. Part of the reason for this, according to the
Addiction Research Foundation of Ontario, is the difference in

male and female drinking habits: "Women alcoholics, for example, tend to be spree drinkers, whereas men, who can still drink somewhat more openly without social disapproval, are more likely to be continuous drinkers. Researchers have found that unremittent drinking patterns are much more strongly associated with cirrhosis than the 'bender' style of drinking."

But beyond the differences in the *way* women and men drink there are physiological and biological differences that play a very important part in how alcohol is handled and the way it affects the individual woman. Some of the differences may very well be beneficial. The female kidney, for example, is only 82 percent the weight of the male's, and thus appears to function more efficiently. Because the kidneys play a role in expelling alcohol from the body (in the urine), this could be a plus. On the other hand, while women under age 35 have slightly lower blood pressure than men, once they reach 40 or 45, both systolic and diastolic pressures rise at a greater rate than in males, probably because of the hormonal changes of menopause. (Systolic pressure, represented by the higher number, is the force with which the blood is pumped by the heart during the period it contracts; diastolic pressure is the force with which the blood is pumped by the heart during relaxation.)

While there is some good evidence that alcohol in moderate amounts may lower the risk of heart attack, lessen the damaging effects of circulatory problems, and control high blood pressure, all the evidence is not yet in on whether alcohol damages the heart and circulation or decreases or increases the blood flow through the heart's vessels. Thus, a woman's propensity to higher blood pressure in later life, coupled with any medications she may require to control it, could spell trouble in the way her body reacts to alcohol in unreasonable amounts.

But before examining any more of the physiological differences that put women at odds with alcohol, and some of the special effects it has on them, some information about the chemi-

cal nature and action of the substance under discussion might
be helpful.

It's important to know that beverage alcohol is still
C_2H_5OH, ethanol, to the metabolism of women and men, and
that despite the variations in how the sexes respond to it, its
basic mechanism, once in the bloodstream, is generally quite
the same. Ethanol, or ethyl alcohol, is a natural, colorless, and
flammable substance produced when fermenting sugar reacts
with yeast spores.

Among the beverages laced with alcohol, beer and ale have
the lowest amount; beer has between 4 and 4.5 percent, ale has
a bit more, and malt liquor has around 6 percent. The popular
dinner wines—Zinfandel, Burgundy, Chianti, and Chablis—
have between 10 and 14 percent alcohol, and the so-called for-
tified wines (sherry, port, and marsala) contain between 17 and
20 percent, a substantial amount of which has been added,
sometimes in the form of brandy. Distilled, or hard, liquor,
such as gin, vodka, scotch, rum, and liqueurs, contains more concentrated alcohol, anywhere from 40 to 75 percent. The quantity of alcohol in any given distilled liquor is expressed on the
label as "proof," the actual amount of alcohol in the drink being
one-half the proof number. Thus, 100-proof vodka is 50 percent alcohol, and 86-proof whiskey equals 43 percent alcohol.
The strongest liquors available in the United States, 151-proof
bourbon and rum, contain about 75 percent alcohol.

Pharmacologically, alcohol is classified as a drug that de-
presses the central nervous system, much as barbiturates, sedatives, and anesthetics do. It is not, as most people believe, a
stimulant, and the popular image of the St. Bernard plodding
toward a snowbound victim with a rejuvenating cask of rum
hanging from its neck is more for cartoons than for reality.
There is no question that after a drink or two an impression of
warmth envelops the drinker and this, along with the tranquility that comes with alcohol in moderation, might be of some
comfort to the frostbitten. And, as drinking progresses, the

drinker is stimulated to a certain degree: Speech becomes free
and animated, social inhibitions may be lost, and the drinker
may even begin to act more emotionally. But these effects are,
for the most part, false. The warmth that seems to flow through
your body when you drink is really on the surface of the skin.
As the alcohol you've drunk is oxidized, the excess is picked up
by the blood and brought to the skin, where it is released by
nerves and enlarged capillaries.

As far as the "stimulation" (the talkativeness and loss of in-
hibition) is concerned, this occurs only because alcohol affects
those portions of your brain that control your judgment and re-
straints. What you regard as being stimulated actually amounts
to a depression of your self-control that manifests itself in loud
and rapid conversation or aggressive and uninhibited behavior.
Thus, the principal effect of alcohol is to slow down brain activity, and depending on what, how much, and how fast you
drink, the ultimate result is slurred speech, hazy thinking,
slowed reaction time, dulled hearing, impaired vision,
weakened muscles, and fogged memory. Certainly not a description of what caffeine and nicotine, both stimulants, will do
to you.

Alcohol is also classified as a food because it contains ener-
gizing calories. As most drinkers know, the average cocktail has
as many of those weight-producing units as a potato. But there
the similarity ends. Unlike a potato or any other food, alcohol
has no nutritional value whatsoever. The calories are empty,
and you wouldn't be able to live for very long on such energy,
nor more than you could on sugar and soda. Alcohol is also not
digested as other foods are. Instead of being converted by
blood plasma and transported to our cells and tissues, where it
would be of benefit if it were a real food, it avoids all of the
complicated digestive processes and gets right to the point. In
two minutes it's coursing through the bloodstream. About 20
percent of the alcohol you consume in an average drink is absorbed directly into the blood through the stomach walls and

rushes straight for the brain and other organs and tissues. The remainder is processed a bit slower through the normal gastrointestinal system.

The effects of alcohol are, naturally, determined by its strength. It gets diluted by the water volume of the body—in the blood and in the organs it affects, such as the liver—in order to facilitate its transmission throughout the system. Those vital organs (like the brain, which controls memory, balance, and coordination, among other things) that contain a lot of water and need an ample blood supply are particularly vulnerable. Dilution does, however, cut the alcohol's potency somewhat, and here is where one important biological difference between men and women comes into play: Muscle tissue contains more water than fat tissue, so men—who have more muscle and less fat than women—have about 10 percent more water in their bodies, which means that alcohol gets diluted more in a man's system than in a woman's. Therefore, if a man and woman consume an equal amount of liquor, the woman is more likely to be adversely affected. This disparity is noted even if the woman weighs the same as the man. Moreover, the fact that in most populations the woman's brain is, on the average, 10 percent smaller than the male's means that there is even less water in a woman's body to dilute the alcohol in the organ where it works most of its interference.

Weight and body size are, of course, important to the speed at which you burn off alcohol. So, too, are your hormone levels, as we will see later. These factors, along with whether there is food in your stomach to slow absorption of the alcohol, how fast you drink, what you drink, and the setting in which you drink, determine just how quickly alcohol affects the brain and the rest of your vital organs. Weight, in fact, provides some dramatic evidence of alcohol's fickle nature. In most cases, if you drink the same amount of liquor that a heavier person does, you'll feel it more, and quicker. The example that is commonly used is that a 180-pound man can drink three ounces of 86-proof liquor or sixteen ounces of beer in two hours without too much of a jolt to his system. The accepted rule is that for every 20 pounds over or under the 180, add or subtract one-half ounce. Using that scale, a 220-pounder could safely drink four ounces of liquor in two hours, but someone weighing 140 would have to settle for two ounces.

This puts women at somewhat of a disadvantage—if you consider being able to drink someone under the table an advantage. As we have said, women generally have less muscle mass than men and a smaller bone structure, and though some women are heavier because they have more fat, this doesn't compensate enough to allow them to drink as much as a man. This is because fat tissue doesn't have enough water to dilute the alcohol. It is the size of the frame that counts. So, unless you have a large frame and you're carrying around a lot of muscle, the prudent course is to drink less than a man, holding consumption to around one drink or less per hour. The obese woman with excess fat tissue must also be extremely careful about how much she drinks and ought to get into the habit of diluting drinks with water to compensate for the lower water content in her tissue.

Your emotional state also affects the way you handle alcohol. If, for example, you are emotionally upset or tired, the alcohol may make matters worse, just as tranquilizers, in some individuals, may bring on the paradoxical reactions of depression and anxiety. If you should have postpartum blues, for instance, or are tense during your premenstrual stage, careless drinking is certainly not the way out. Some premenstrual women, too, show signs of increased libido during that phase. If the theories about women feeling sexier when they drink are correct, then overdoing alcohol at a time of low hormone levels—a problem in itself—could raise further considerations that are, depending on your point of view, a plus or a minus. (You should also be aware that alcohol does, indeed, as the porter in *Macbeth* said, "provoke" desire in men because of the action of liquor on hormone levels. It is, however, equally true that liquor "unprovokes"—it takes away the performance.)

It's good to remember, also, that the mind-body relationship is a close one when it comes to alcohol: If, when you're drinking, you're convinced that drunkenness will occur, chances are that it will happen more easily than if you aren't thinking much about it. It's somewhat like bringing on a stomach ulcer by worrying about getting one.

Almost as soon as the alcohol you consume gets into your bloodstream, your automatic disposal system is switched on. Nearly 90 percent of this detoxification takes place in your liver by the aforementioned enzyme, ADH. The rest is expelled directly from the lungs when you exhale, and through the kidneys and urine, in saliva, tears, and sweat. While it's not a crucial point in discussing how alcohol affects women, the fact that women have a lower perspiration rate than men is noteworthy when considering comfort while drinking. The physiologic responses of women to hot environments are said to differ from those of men, possibly because of hormones, body build, or behavioral patterns. Women supposedly are less able to cope with heat; if this is true, the combination of the heat that alcohol releases when it is oxidized in the liver and transported to the skin, and the inability to use a natural cooling mechanism as efficiently as men could add up to discomfort when drinking under certain conditions.

In general, it takes about an hour for the body to oxidize the alcohol in an average cocktail, say a 12-ounce can of beer or a 4-ounce glass of wine—all of which, incidentally, contain the same amount of alcohol. This means that as long as you don't have more than one drink an hour, the disposal system will work efficiently and the effects will be moderate. There is, of course, individual variation, which may be as high as 50 percent more or less than the average. Women, because their basal metabolic rate (the amount of energy expended when at rest) is 6 to 10 percent lower than that of men of the same size and age, might expel alcohol at a slower rate and thus could remain drunk longer than men from equal amounts of liquor.

Bearing in mind the different rates at which women and men metabolize alcohol and the individual variations, there are some rough statements to make about the effects of given quantities on the system of both sexes. For instance, when the concentration of alcohol in your bloodstream is 0.05 percent or less, you begin to experience the feeling of warmth and tranquility associated with the pleasure of drinking. Depending on how much liquor is in your drink, on how fast you consume it and on the other factors cited, this state is achieved after one to three cocktails or large cans of beer. With this amount of alcohol in your blood, your inhibitions may be lessened and your judgment affected, but you are legally sober. (This doesn't mean, however, that your ability to operate a car won't be impaired: One survey by the National Transportation Safety Board found that the chances of a driver causing a highway accident increased at a lower level.)

With increasing liquor intake, there is a noticeable decrease in your muscle control and an increase in reaction time—the time it takes for a muscle to respond to a signal from the brain. There is some evidence suggesting that, after a few drinks, women tend to have a somewhat longer reaction time than men. Highway accident statistics, for instance, indicate that drinking women involved in automobile mishaps have lower blood-alcohol levels than men who have experienced similar accidents. One might infer from this that women may be more sensitive to alcohol-induced deficiencies than men.

After six or seven cocktails, your blood alcohol level is around 0.15 percent—a state of definite intoxication. Most drinkers with that much alcohol in their systems are unable to walk, see clearly, judge distances, or control their emotions, and it could take as long as ten hours to sober up. At 0.25 percent, which is registered after drinking about twelve ounces of liquor in a few hours, there is vomiting and loss of comprehension. At

0.30 percent, the drinker is in total confusion, and at 0.40 percent, body temperature drops drastically, heart action and blood pressure slow up, and unconsciousness and perhaps even death can occur.

The steady and inevitable progression from euphoria to fuzzy thinking to unconsciousness that occurs as the brain becomes more and more saturated with alcohol cannot always be charted precisely because, as has been pointed out, various circumstances govern the mechanism of metabolism. But what is important to remember is that, relatively speaking, only a tiny amount of alcohol—one-half of 1 percent—can be lethal.

Scientists have also begun to look into the effects of various drinks on individual behavior, focusing on substances called congeners that are in all alcoholic beverages. Congeners, such as fusel oil, tannin, acetic acid and aldehydes, are the by-products of fermentation or appear when wooden casks are used to age beverages. They are actually what make an alcoholic beverage a whiskey, vodka or wine, giving each of these drinks their own special color, taste, and odor. A good rule to remember is that the higher the congener count in a beverage, the darker the color and the heavier the odor and taste. Although scientists aren't too sure how congeners affect drinkers, there is some evidence to suggest that people who drink beverages with higher congener content, such as whiskey, take more risks than those who drink vodka or gin.

Alcohol's effects are not, of course, manifested only in our coordination, gait, and speech. Cirrhosis of the liver has already been mentioned, and we know that there is a connection between cirrhosis and liver cancer: Possibly as many as 90 percent of all liver malignancies begin in cirrhotic livers. There is mixed opinion as to whether alcohol harms or helps the heart. However, there is no question that alcohol can have an adverse effect on the digestive and reproductive systems, on sexual function, on the fetus of a pregnant woman who drinks, and on the very basic unit of life itself, the cell. There are physiological effects, too, when alcohol is combined with cigarettes and other drugs. Most people who drink heavily also smoke heavily, and researchers have suggested that the risk of developing cancer of the mouth and throat is much greater than if they did neither. Alcohol combined with tranquilizers, antihistamines, birth control pills, and anticoagulants presents another set of problems.

But before we look at some of these clinical consequences, we wish to repeat a point we made at the outset and which will be made throughout this book: Unabused, alcohol is not a problem. Moderate drinking is not going to destroy your body or your psyche—unless, of course, you are an alcoholic—and it may well do you some good. When we talk of the behavioral and physical disturbances associated with alcohol, we are talking about the sustained, heavy use that is a way of life for the alcoholic and the problem drinker. We are not talking about the sort of responsible drinking in which the vast majority of Americans engage.

ALCOHOL AND THE BODY

Let's take a look, first, at how alcohol affects your gastrointestinal (GI) tract, the system made up of your stomach and intestines. In moderate amounts, alcohol doesn't appear to irritate the delicate mucosa that lines the GI tract, unless the drinker has a stomach disorder, such as an ulcer. In that case, even small amounts of liquor may stimulate enough gastric acid to aggravate the ulcer. Occasional overindulgence often results in nothing more serious than nausea, vomiting, and diarrhea. But the regular consumption of excessive amounts of alcohol can touch off attacks of gastritis, esophagitis, and pancreatitis.

Gastritis, an inflammation of the lining of the stomach, arises from excess acidity and is often accompanied by severe bleeding. The condition is not uncommon in binge drinkers. Gastroenterologists have also found that, when alcohol enters the intestines from the stomach, it stimulates the production of fatty substances that find their way into the bloodstream and lead to a condition called fatty liver. These substances also boost production of cholesterol, a fatty alcohol, in the blood and this, as most of us know, has been strongly associated with atherosclerosis, or hardening of the arteries, a condition arising when excessive amounts of cholesterol plug the arteries.

The expression, "Down the hatch," if acted upon too often, can result in an inflammation of the lining of the esophagus, the twelve-inch food pipe that extends from the back of the throat to the stomach. Continual irritation from alcohol, other drugs, and cigarette smoking can cause the condition known as esophagitis, and although it is curable, by ingesting a bland diet and antacids, the discomfort it causes—severe burning pain and difficulty in swallowing—makes for another convincing case against the heavy use of liquor.

More serious is acute pancreatitis, an inflammation of the large glandular organ that lies behind the stomach. The pancreas secretes enzymes for digestion into the intestines and manufactures insulin, necessary for proper utilization of sugar. The evidence is fairly convincing that heavy alcohol consumption can have a direct toxic effect on the pancreas, due primarily to the increased digestive acids and enzymes drinking produces and which overwhelm and damage it. Diabetes, characterized by the body's inability to burn up sugar, can also result if insulin production falls off. This condition, for which there is good treatment available, can be most disastrous for the alcoholic. Not only is there a special problem if the diabetic drinks heavy amounts of wines high in sugar, such as kosher and dessert wines, but she or he might neglect a proper diet, or forget to take the necessary insulin. Diabetic acidosis and coma, with signs that include flushed skin, drowsy behavior, deep labored breathing, and nausea and vomiting, may result. On the other hand, if the diabetic takes too much insulin, she or he might experience a sudden reaction marked by shakiness and unsteady gait, slurred speech, laughing or crying without cause, light-headedness, and possibly loss of consciousness. It's fairly obvious that if the diabetic who shows either of these reactions is in a drinking environment, chances are good that the symptoms will be mistaken for intoxication, and the necessary emergency measures might not be taken until it's too late.

With regard to alcohol's effects on the cardiovascular system, it is known that moderate amounts slightly increase the heart rate and dilate blood vessels in the legs, arms, and skin. Blood pressure may rise, but it generally drops when the sedative effect of the liquor takes hold. Recent studies have also shown that when heavy amounts of alcohol are consumed, they may damage the thick muscular wall of the heart, the myocardium. The resulting condition is called alcoholic cardiomyopathy or, as it is popularly known, alcoholic heart disease. At Boston's Lemuel Shattuck Hospital a few years ago, Dr. David H. Spodick of Tufts Medical School studied twenty-six alcoholics who had been drinking a quart of liquor a day and who had no previous clinical signs of heart trouble. He found that their heart action was less efficient because of myocardial damage. Researchers are uncertain how alcohol affects the heart muscle. Some studies suggest that there is a direct toxic effect—feeding pure alcohol to mice, for example, can produce direct heart muscle damage. Others suggest that alcohol activates a virus that is responsible; still others, that liquor indirectly injures the heart muscle by throwing nutrition off-track.

We said earlier that alcohol provides no nutritional value other than empty calories. Because alcoholics tend to drink more than they eat, they are apt to develop a wide range of diseases related to a diet deficient in the essential proteins and vitamins. One of these is cirrhosis. Although the disease occurs in nondrinkers as well—vitamin B deficiency, viruses, syphilis, overexposure to certain toxic chemicals, excessive consumption of sugar and soft drinks have all been implicated as causes—it shows up about eight times more often in alcoholics. While nutritional deficiencies, particularly of the B vitamins, have long been associated with alcoholic liver disease, there is a wide difference of opinion about the role diet plays in its cause. Some researchers feel that a well-balanced diet is a defense against cirrhosis, others that large amounts of alcohol will injure the liver even if the diet is adequate. (It is generally accepted that if you drink 80 to 100 gm of alcohol a day for five to ten years, chances are you'll develop liver disease. This amounts to about a half pint of whiskey, eight beers or a liter of wine a day.) Whatever the relationship between liver disease and alcohol, it's certain that heavy drinkers who don't eat well are running the double risk of nutritional problems and a liver disorder.

Another disorder, one that causes mental deterioration, is alcoholic pellagra, a vitamin deficiency disease due to a lack of niacin, one of the B vitamins. Yet another is Korsakoff's psychosis, a mental affliction characterized by loss of memory, disorientation, and auditory hallucinations. One interesting reaction is that the sufferer devises elaborate systems for justifying untruths and will offer any kind of answer in an effort to cover up the memory defect. Although the disease is seen as a result of chronic alcoholism, it is due chiefly to a thiamine and niacin deficiency. Treatment, in fact, consists of daily doses of thiamine chloride, powdered yeast in iced milk, and a diet rich in all nutrients.

ALCOHOL AND MENOPAUSE

Alcohol has a number of other clinical effects, among them one known as osteoporosis that is particularly troubling to menopausal women. It results from a low calcium level. Because it affects the pituitary gland—the linchpin of the hormone-secreting endocrine system—alcohol may disturb growth and development and upset the delicate balance of water and minerals. During periods of heavy alcohol consumption, magnesium, an element vital to the body's chemistry, is depleted. Since magnesium maintains the electrical activity— and thus the ability to function—of nerves and muscles and has a strong influence on the central nervous system, its loss may be partly responsible for some of the emotional and muscular symptoms that accompany drinking. Alcohol thus appears to interfere with absorption of calcium, essential to bones, teeth, and blood plasma. A low calcium level in the blood not only causes the muscles to go into painful spasm, a condition known as tetany, but can produce the brittleness and softness of bones known as osteoporosis.

If a woman alcoholic is also experiencing menopause, chances are she'll weaken her bones even more. It's been suggested, in fact, that the bone structure of alcoholic women in their 40s is similar in density to that of women in their 70s. The menopausal woman also might find that smaller amounts of alcohol are affecting her—that is, she might get fuzzier or drunk quicker than she did in her youth, or she might find that one drink is making her nervous and agitated, maybe even troubled by lower self-esteem.

This could possibly have something to do with calcium depletion in another of its characteristics: its role as a regulator of nerve and muscle excitability. The late Adelle Davis explained it this way: "Calcium is used by the nerves in the transportation of impulses. When calcium is undersupplied, nerves become tense and irritable. . . . The calcium-deficient adult is inclined to be quick-tempered, grouchy and irritable, and to have a feeling of tenseness and uneasiness. . . ."[1] This is not necessarily the answer, but it is well known that many menopausal women are anxious and uneasy.

Regardless of what causes the anxiety—calcium depletion or reduction in estrogen production—there's little doubt that it can be aggravated by alcohol. For some people, even a single drink makes them aggressive and hostile, even depressed. Drinking, instead of tranquilizing and easing anxiety as it does in most drinkers, actually makes the woman feel worse. If the menopausal woman experienced such a reaction before the onset of her change, she is well advised to be careful about how she drinks.

ALCOHOL AND DRUGS

There is yet another, much more serious consequence of alcohol use, one that does not require heavy drinking to bring about. It has to do with what can happen when you mix certain prescription or nonprescription medications with alcoholic beverages. A case in point involves a mildly diabetic woman on Orinase (tolbutamide), an oral antidiabetic drug. Before lunch one afternoon, she had a glass of wine. "The reaction between the two was almost immediate," her husband wrote the U.S. Food and Drug Administration. "She passed into a condition of shock and almost lost consciousness, becoming violently ill."

It's pretty common knowledge that we are a pill-popping, elixer-taking society, spending $8.5 billion for prescription drugs in 1977. That rounds out to an average of six prescriptions a year for every individual. That year we also spent $3.8 billion for over-the-counter (OTC) medications to take care of our heartburn and headaches, sore throats and sleeplessness. But the problem isn't just that we take all these pills and potions, but that we generally don't know much about how they work, either alone or in combination with other drugs or with alcohol. You should be aware that there are some 30,000 prescription drugs on the market, along with a bewildering assortment of 100,000 OTC preparations, and each one has some potential side effect, mild or serious.

Although not every drug is at odds with alcohol, it's good

to remember that of the 100 most frequently prescribed drugs—and a great many OTC preparations—more than half contain at least one ingredient that can react adversely with your cocktail, small glass of lunchtime vermouth, or "harmless" bottle of light beer. These alcohol-medication interactions range from the drowsy feeling that comes with combining a drink with antihistamine-containing allergy pills, to possible death when you mix a cocktail with the phenobarbital in your prescription sleeping pills.

A woman is more likely than a man to experience one of these drug-alcohol reactions, not necessarily because her metabolism is different, but simply because she is the prime consumer of prescription medicine and has been for years. A woman's complex reproductive role, and a physiology that causes female disorders to outnumber those of the male by four to one, may be one reason. Another is the fact that as a group, women suffer a good deal of stress, much of it, as we have seen, quite different from that faced by men. And for this reason, more women than men might seek a doctor for mood-altering drugs. Women were top consumers of the patent medicines so popular in the nineteenth and early twentieth centuries. One concoction, Lydia Pinkham's Vegetable Compound, was 18 to 21 percent alcohol. Billed as a "positive cure for all those complaints and weaknesses so common to our best female population," it grossed almost $4 million in 1925.

Perhaps women's closeness to medicine is rooted in their traditional nurturing role. According to historian Will Durant, ". . . they made midwifery, rather than venality, the oldest profession . . . because their closer connection with the soil gave them a superior knowledge of plants, and enabled them to develop the art of medicine."[2]

Whatever the reasons, women are no strangers to medication, and they have remained the principal users of certain prescription medicines—notably tranquilizers, hormones, amphetamines, and barbiturate-containing sleeping pills. More than 30 million women in the United States, according to the National Institute of Drug Abuse, have taken tranquilizers, compared to 18 million men. Eighty percent of amphetamine prescriptions are written for women, and of the 25 million sleeping pills prescribed every year in this country, two-thirds end up with women. Nearly 100 million women in the world, some 15 million in the United States, use combination estrogen-progestin birth control pills.

Whether women get more prescriptions for psychotropic drugs than men because of behavior that's been called "learned helplessness," because they're more likely to discuss their emotional problems, or because of the physician's traditional paternalistic attitude, is not an easy question to answer. What is important is that in light of the statistics on use, the fuller the medicine chest, the higher the probability of an interaction between drugs. Moreover, since many women drink, the danger of an interaction with alcohol is heightened. Add a third strike against woman—her different physiological and metabolic makeup—and there's a good chance she'll wind up an overdose patient in a hospital emergency room more often than a man. The names of the late Dorothy Kilgallen and Marilyn Monroe, and comatose Karen Ann Quinlan come immediately to mind when one talks of mixing alcohol and medication, and it is interesting to note that in each of these three cases where pills were combined with liquor, no one drug had been taken in sufficient quantity to cause death or coma. What's frightening is that an amount of alcohol that cannot possibly harm you and a sleeping pill that is also not lethal alone can, when taken together, kill you: One Valium with one can of beer can pack the punch of close to a dozen tranquilizers.

Combinations of drugs and alcohol interact in different ways. Sometimes, alcohol has a direct effect on the pharmacologic effect of a medicine, either enhancing its strength in the body, or decreasing the effectiveness of the drug. Other times, alcohol alters the body chemistry so that essential medication is either blocked from doing its job, or has its activity in the body dangerously speeded up.

Before we look at some specific alcohol-drug interactions, bear in mind that drugs, for all of their potential for harm, do sustain health and life. Most drugs are, of course, not toxic in themselves and to suggest that we are being systematically poisoned by physicians and pharmaceutical manufacturers would be the height of irresponsibility. But when you take a medication, it's important to know something about how it works and how risky it is. So, too, should your doctor. He or she should also be aware of what other drugs you are taking, whether or not you're a drinker, heavy or otherwise, and what other ailments you have.

Adverse drug reactions are a fact of life, and they occur, as Senator Kennedy has charged, because too many physicians prescribe too many drugs on the basis of too little information. According to one estimate, at least 16,000 deaths a year are related to such drug reactions, and perhaps as many as 120,000. Information from the Drug Abuse Warning Network (DAWN) indicates that more than 47,000 people who drink in combination with other drugs are treated in hospital emergency rooms each year—and more than 2,500 deaths occur each year because of such combinations.

Let's examine a few that you should know about.

A broad category called *central nervous system depressants* includes all the agents that calm or sedate you, the "downers" that relieve tension and anxiety. Each can make you drowsy, impair your coordination, and decrease your alertness, and in this regard they behave almost like alcohol, which is also, as we have said, a CNS depressant. Mix alcohol with any of them and you will compound their effect, perhaps lowering your perception and alertness to a danger point and slowing you so much that you drop deeper into stupor, and then death can occur.

Barbiturates—drugs like Phenobarbital, Luminal, Seconal, Nembutal, Doriden, Pentothal, Butisol, and Amytal—are classified as CNS depressants. There are also close to 100 different combinations of barbiturates, and alone or in combination, they are widely prescribed to induce sleep, alleviate jitters, and prevent epileptic seizures. One study cited by the National Institute of Alcohol Abuse and Alcoholism found that the lethal dose of barbiturates was almost 50 percent lower when the drugs are taken with alcohol than when taken alone. Overdosing, then, doesn't have to be a factor. Nor do you have to drink and take the drugs simultaneously to trigger the extra depressant effect. Studies have demonstrated again and again that if you take even a short-acting barbiturate several hours before you drink, there's a fairly good chance you'll fall asleep or experience difficulty with motor skills.

The so-called minor tranquilizers are also CNS depressants. This category includes Valium, Miltown, Librium, and Equanil. There are also the major tranquilizers, antipsychotics used to treat serious emotional disturbances, such as Thorazine, Mellaril, Prolixin, Haldol, and Serpasil. No tranquilizer should ever be taken with alcohol, least of all the "majors": Karen Ann Quinlan's ill-fated combination included Valium, Librium, barbiturates, aspirin, quinine, and alcohol. The FDA has warned that a person who takes this class of tranquilizers and also drinks risks severe depression of central nervous system functions, which in turn can seriously impair voluntary movements such as walking or using the hands. The combination can also produce a severe and possibly fatal depression of the respiratory system, not to mention increasing the possibility of liver damage.

A recent theory explaining how the major tranquilizers work adds to the caution of mixing them with liquor. According to the theory, a brain chemical, dopamine, involved in the transmission of nerve impulses is blocked by the tranquilizers. Since dopamine is responsible for stimulating the portions of the brain that control emotion and inhibit various muscular activities, rendering it ineffective results in runaway emotions, mental illness, and involuntary movements. Recently, scientists at the Veterans Administration Hospital in Houston found that large amounts of alcohol might also inhibit the way dopamine works. Instead of performing as it usually does, dopamine is converted, in the presence of alcohol, into a chemical called THP, which happens to be the intermediate chemical in poppies that leads to the synthesis of morphine. It should be obvious, then, that mixing two powerful agents that directly affect an essential brain chemical is quite foolhardy.

Nonbarbiturate hypnotics—Doriden, Quaalude, Placidyl, chloral hydrate, Sopor, and Dalmane—are also CNS depressants. Methaqualone, which is the principal ingredient in Quaalude and Sopor, is prescribed as a sleep aid, but it is also heavily abused by drug addicts. Taken alone, it impairs the ability to drive or operate machinery. Taken with alcohol, it may be incapacitating. A mixture of alcohol and chloral hydrate, the ingredient in Noctec, a sedating agent, can literally knock you off your feet and put you into a long sleep. This combination, known for years as a Mickey Finn, can cause rapid heartbeat, flushing, and headaches, especially dangerous problems for someone with heart disease.

It's also important to know that while some of the nonbarbiturates like Dalmane apparently do not depress the "sleep center" of the brain as directly as the barbiturates, they do remain in the body longer—several days, in fact—thus making them more available to the effects of alcohol. Even taking a drink the day after taking the drug can impair ability to drive.

A number of agents that are generally inhaled— amyl nitrate, nitrous oxide (laughing gas), the Freon gas in aerosol sprays, and airplane glue—are also CNS depressants. So, too, are the narcotics: codeine, Demerol, heroin, methadone, morphine, opium, and Percodan. Antihistamines, widely used in OTC allergy preparations, cough and cold remedies, and sleep and motion sickness aids, also have an effect on the central nervous system. Interestingly, though, they can both depress and stimulate it, and have other opposite effects, such as causing constipation and diarrhea, sluggishness and euphoria. Such varying effects make the drugs' action when combined with alcohol even more unpredictable, and it's good advice to take the "milder" OTC medications as seriously as you do your prescription drugs when it comes to mixing them with any other drug. One cold capsule with a cocktail can double the effect of a drink in an average-sized man, and perhaps triple or quadruple it in a woman.

A class of drugs called monoamine oxidase (MAO) inhibitors (Eutonyl, Nardil, Marplan, and Parnate) are *stimulants* used to treat depression and hypertension. These present special problems because they can react with alcohol, with certain foods, and with other drugs. Chianti wines, sherry, and beer, for example, contain a substance called tyramine, which, when mixed with an MAO inhibitor can sharply increase blood pressure to bring on hypertensive crisis or cause severe headaches and brain hemorrhage. Foods such as aged cheese, pepperoni, salami, chocolate, chicken liver, and pickled herring also contain tyramine, and patients on MAO inhibitors should not eat such products. Antihistamines and amphetamines (the latter are stimulants) also react with the antidepressants.

A word here about a nonprescription drug that is widely used and is no stranger to women, especially adolescents—marijuana. Recently, scientists at the Research Institute on Alcoholism in Buffalo suggested that prolonged use of alcohol with marijuana may have more detrimental consequences than the use of either drug alone. Basing their conclusion on animal studies, the researchers found that when the active ingredient in marijuana, tetrahydrocannabinol (THC), is given with alcohol to rats, it increases the rate at which alcohol tolerance and physical dependence develop. The incidence of body tremors following drug withdrawal, they discovered, was greater in the THC-plus-alcohol rats than in the animals given alcohol alone. Rats treated with both THC and alcohol were also highly aggressive during drug withdrawal, while those treated only with alcohol were docile in comparison. Control animals and animals treated only with THC showed no signs of physical drug dependence.

Pain-killers, both prescription and OTC, may also interact unpleasantly with alcohol. Aspirin, for instance, can cause stomach bleeding in some individuals, including those with a history of ulcers. Alcohol also acts as an irritant, and can aggravate this effect. The aspirin substitute acetaminophen, the ingredient in more than 200 nonprescription drugs, the most common of which is Tylenol, can also cause problems and even death when mixed with alcohol.

According to Dr. Craig J. McClain, a liver disease specialist at the University of Minnesota, alcohol boosts acetaminophen's ability to produce serious liver failure. McClain and his colleagues at the Minneapolis Veterans Administration Hospital recently studied three patients with the condition, each of whom drank a pint of whiskey a day. The three had also taken at least five to fifteen grams of acetaminophen a day for one to three days. (The maximum safe daily dosage of the analgesic, according to the FDA, is four grams.) One of the three died and, according to McClain, death was not due to a cirrhotic liver but to massive hepatic damage brought on by the combination. Alcohol, the physicians reported, stimulates production of a liver enzyme that increases the amount of a toxic byproduct of the analgesic. This byproduct, not yet chemically identified, destroys liver cells.

Although McClain's patients were very heavy drinkers, the internist feels that heavy social drinkers might also be at risk. Many drinkers, in fact, favor acetaminophen as a hangover remedy because it lacks the gastric side effects of aspirin. "Although less likely to cause death," McClain reported, "anyone who drinks from three to four shots a day could end up with a certain amount of liver damage if they also take large doses of acetaminophen."[3]

The prescription analgesics are usually opiates, either derivatives of morphine or synthetics. One of these opiate-like pain-killers is propoxyphene, sold chiefly under the trade names Darvon, Darvon Compound, Darvon-N, and Darvocet-N. A popular prescription item, accounting for more than $150 million in retail sales a year, propoxyphene has caused numerous deaths, many of them attributed to its use in combination with alcohol or other drugs. According to the American Medical Association, fifteen to twenty Darvon tablets can cause death, but when the analgesic is taken with alcohol or other drugs, only a few tablets might be dangerous.

At one time, former HEW Secretary Joseph A. Califano reportedly considered banning propoxyphene as a health hazard, but ultimately asked the FDA to decide whether its use ought to be restricted. In July 1979, the FDA announced that Darvon's manufacturer, Eli Lilly & Company, would begin distributing a consumer leaflet warning of the hazards of taking the drug in excess or with alcoholic beverages and other drugs. Lilly also agreed to add new warnings about Darvon to the information it provides physicians. The consumer leaflet warns patients that the use of Darvon—a safe drug when used properly—in combination with tranquilizers, sleep aids, antidepressants, antihistamines, or other drugs that make a person sleepy could increase their effects and lead to symptoms of overdose. It adds: "An overdose of Darvon, alone or in combination with other drugs, including alcohol, may cause weakness, difficulty in breathing, confusion, anxiety, and more severe drowsiness and dizziness. Extreme overdosage may lead to unconsciousness and death."

Many drug-takers also perform chemical balancing acts. For instance, the person who abuses amphetamines (Benzedrine, Dexedrine, Methedrine, and Preludin) will often combine them with barbiturates in an effort to wind down the "speed run" that the stimulants induce. Or, a psychiatrist might prescribe amphetamines in combination with sedatives to reduce the drowsiness. Such mixtures, when medically indicated and carefully managed, can benefit the patient. But taking a stimulant—even a milder one like coffee—with alcohol in the mistaken belief that it will offset the effects of the drink can present serious problems. Suppose, for example, that a drinker reacts to alcohol by becoming aggressive and overly emotional. She decides to take one of the amphetamines her doctor prescribed when she was dieting, reasoning that it will increase her alertness and bring her back to a more normal state. Actually, exactly the opposite can occur. The amphetamine, because it is a stimulant that not only heightens awareness but excites, may magnify the aggressive behavior to such an extent that the drinker becomes violent. As one physician put it, "In some people, several drinks lower inhibitions so that the person wants to do things they ordinarily wouldn't do. When they take speed drugs with the booze, they've now got the gas to do them." Taking stimulants with alcohol also might give the drinker a false sense of security when she tries to drive. Again, drug interactions are not easy to predict, given all the variables of quantity, individual metabolism, and chemical composition of the drug; using one to counter the effects of another, unless you're a highly skilled clinician, is not advisable.

Anticoagulants, also, are affected by alcohol, which can interfere with some of the blood's clotting factors. If you are taking medications such as Panwarfin, Dicumarol, Sintrom or Coumadin—agents prescribed to prevent blood clots in veins and lung arteries—drinking can increase the blood-thinning effects of the drugs. Most other drugs—barbiturates, antibiotics, tranquilizers, diuretics, hormones, and salicylates—also react in some way with anticoagulants and should be taken with great care.

Diabetics on insulin may find that drinking increases the activity of their medication, producing an unexpected drop in blood sugar. Mixing alcohol with diuretics, drugs taken to help rid the body of excess fluid, can cause a reduction in blood pressure, producing dizziness when an individual stands up. Flagyl, which is used to treat vaginal infections, Fulvicin, used for ringworm, and Chloromycetin, a wide-spectrum antibiotic used to fight serious infections, are antimicrobial drugs that actually interfere with the metabolism of alcohol itself. Thus, a person who drinks and takes one of these drugs runs a risk of a reaction somewhat akin to that experienced by heavy drinkers who are prescribed the drug Antabuse to break their habit. When a drinker takes Antabuse, even a tiny amount of alcohol brings on difficulty in breathing, throbbing pain in the head, vomiting, sweating, and a rapid heartbeat. The reaction lasts about thirty minutes to an hour, but the Antabuse remains in the system for as long as two weeks. During that period, almost any quantity of alcohol that is drunk will touch off a reaction severe enough to discourage drinking, at least theoretically.

ALCOHOL AND THE PILL

One of the greatest medication dilemmas facing women today involves estrogen, the female sex hormone. This is an especially nettling issue because so many women are exposed to this hormone for so much of their adult life, from its use as an oral contraceptive to its use to treat certain gynecological disorders and menopausal symptoms. On one hand, it is a therapeutic blessing. Preparations containing estrogen alleviate hot flashes and vaginal changes such as decreased lubrication and elasticity that can make intercourse and urination painful for postmenopausal women. It is used to treat painful menstruation and irregular bleeding, and can help prevent or arrest osteoporosis. And there is no question but that the pill has freed millions of couples from the fear of unwanted pregnancy.

But, as with any potent drug taken over a long period of time, estrogen can have unfavorable effects. It may increase a woman's chances of developing endometrial cancer, a malignancy in the lining of the uterus, and raise the risk of blood clots. The hormone can also elevate triglycerides, fatty substances in the blood that contribute to the buildup of plaque in blood vessels. Women on the pill may develop serious changes in glucose metabolism, or they may find that their bodies aren't using B vitamins properly. And although there is no solid evidence to back it up, there is concern that estrogen increases the likelihood of a woman's developing breast cancer and high blood pressure.

The metabolic processes that operate in all of the body's cells are complex enough to begin with. The addition of such powerful metabolism-altering agents as estrogen only makes these processes become even more complicated. Some women who take the pill have been found to metabolize alcohol more slowly, a situation that could put a strain on the liver if the overload is consistent. Moreover, if a woman drinks, takes the pill, and smokes cigarettes—not an unusual combination by today's standards—she faces a triple threat of elevated triglyceride and cholesterol levels: Each of the three agents is able to stimulate production of the fatty acids. Hardening of the arteries is not such a far-fetched result. And given the fact that estrogen may affect vitamin B metabolism, the link between the hormone and the possibility of a vitamin B deficiency-type alcoholism is also not out of the question.

Interestingly, drinking women who don't take the pill appear to consume more alcohol than women who do. Studies suggest that low levels of estrogen, which would be the case when the pill is not taken and during the premenstrual phase, may contribute to heavier drinking in two ways. First, at low hormone levels alcohol is metabolized more rapidly, thereby requiring more drinking to maintain a given level of intoxication. Second, depressive symptoms, which often accompany low estrogen levels, may temporarily increase drinking in order to relieve the depression. It would appear to be a no-win situation for a drinking woman, on or off the pill. On it, she runs the risk of elevated triglycerides and possible difficulties due to slower alcohol metabolism. Off it, she might drink more.

The menstrual cycle, too, affects your reaction to alcohol in ways that are similar to the reactions the pill effects. For instance, women may become more intoxicated on the same amount of alcohol during the premenstrual period than during the early or middle phases. This is because three days before menstrual bleeding begins, secretion of the hormones estrogen and progesterone stops. Absence of the hormones causes the alcohol to be metabolized more rapidly, and it is sent quickly to the brain. During the first part of the cycle, however, the ovaries step up their production of estrogen and continually increase the output until they quit. Thus, during the first and middle parts of the cycle, when there is more hormone available—just as there is when a woman takes the pill—alcohol is metabolized more slowly.

ALCOHOL AND PREGNANCY

Another aspect of alcohol use and abuse that may be characteristically feminine involves difficulties of the reproductive system. Among males, physical changes do occur in sexual organs after prolonged drinking, and many chronic male alcoholics take on a decidedly feminine appearance. Some scientists have concluded that alcohol itself causes this feminization by weakening the role of the male hormones, just as nonalcoholic liver disease can bring about feminine characteristics by altering the usual liver-controlled hormone balance. As far as women are concerned, the available evidence indicates that heavy drinkers have higher sterility rates, more miscarriages, and a much higher incidence of obstetrical and gynecological problems than do nonalcoholic women. Wilsnack has suggested that the low estrogen levels that may accompany some types of gynecological difficulties may increase a woman's desire for alcohol. She adds, however, that other, more psychological interpretations of alcoholic women's obstetrical and gynecological problems are also possible.

Excessive drinking among women can result, finally, in another serious consequence, one that has been known since Biblical days but not given any scientific validity until 1968 and 1973. The concern is fetal alcohol syndrome (FAS), a condition in which the alcohol drunk by a pregnant woman passes from her bloodstream, through the placenta, and into the fetus, setting the stage for the birth of a mentally or physically deformed child, even one addicted to alcohol.

It wasn't until 1962, when the thalidomide tragedy surfaced, that physicians and researchers began to take seriously the notion that physical and mental defects could be caused in an unborn child if the mother took drugs during the early stages of pregnancy. Thalidomide, thought to be the ideal sedative, was widely sold without prescription in Germany and England. It turned out to be the most infamous of the defect-causing agents, responsible for thousands of infants being born with deformed or absent limbs. Today, we know that even aspirin, in high doses, has been associated with congenital malformations in the offspring of mothers who took it early in their pregnancies; that a heavy-smoking woman can give birth to an infant who weighs appreciably less than that of a nonsmoking mother; that hormones taken during the first three months of pregnancy can injure the heart of a developing fetus; that diethylstilbestrol, DES, a hormone given to prevent miscarriage, increases the risk of female offspring developing vaginal or cervical cancer.

"For centuries, the fetus, rolling and twisting about in his inland sea inside the mother, has been considered to be quite safely contained within his environment, protected from the cruel world outside by the waters surrounding him and assured of proper nourishment by his direct pipeline to the placenta," Dr. Sidney S. Gellis, an authority on drugs and the fetus and

chairman of the pediatrics department at Tufts–New England
Medical Center, has observed. "This organ was believed to
serve as a very effective barrier to the poisonous substances
which could conceivably reach his body from that of his
mother, witness the ineffectiveness of most agents ingested by
countless generations of women determined to rid themselves
of their unwanted tenants. We now know that the placenta does
not represent the perfect control mechanism we once believed
it to be."[4]

FAS CHILDREN

In 1968, the French researcher P. Lemoine observed 100
children whose mothers were alcoholic and found them to be
mentally deficient. It was the first time that a scientific inves-
tigator had focused on alcohol's effects on the fetus despite the
fact that its properties and action in the body had been known
for years. In 1973, at a conference on genetics and birth defects
held in Boston, Dr. Kenneth L. Jones of the University of
Washington School of Medicine reported that he and his group
had studied eight unrelated children, all of whose mothers
were chronic alcoholics during pregnancy. There was a pattern
of growth deficiency, malformation, and retardation in the
children. Head defects included microcephaly, an abnormally
small head resulting from premature hardening of the skull
and closure of the fontanels, the soft spaces between the bones
of the skull. Their limb joints were abnormal, and they had al-
tered palm crease patterns. There were defects in their hearts,
primarily septal abnormalities in the muscular walls that divided the chambers. Each of the eight was small for his age, and
the average IQ was 63, ranging from below 50 to the middle
70s. Dr. Jones believed that this was the first reported link between maternal alcoholism and any unique malformation pattern in the children.

More recently, investigators have added various skeletal abnormalities to the list of defects. Canadian geneticist Patrick M. MacLeod of the University of British Columbia X-rayed forty-three FAS children and found cervical spine fusions, tapered fingers, and abnormal rib cages. (Congenital heart disease was also discovered in fourteen of the children.) Most of the children's mothers were native Indian women, all extremely heavy drinkers, binging on weekends and having a daily intake of five drinks. "It is important to diagnose the skeletal abnormalities because these children have a greater risk of dislocating their necks in the rough and tumble activities of informal play or gym," he reported.[5]

It is now quite clear that the fetal alcohol syndrome is more than an occasional occurrence, that the ingestion of alcohol by a pregnant woman is one of the most frequent causes of mental deficiency. Investigators are convinced that the damage to the infant is done in utero, and they can point to studies of such children who have been raised in excellent foster homes. These show that the severity of their retardation is identical to that of the children raised by the natural mother.

Researchers have also discovered that mothers who breast feed and drink can cause a pseudo-Cushing's syndrome in their offspring. (The disease, first described in 1932 by Boston neurosurgeon Harvey Cushing, is caused by an overproduction of adrenal hormones. Obesity, a "buffalo hump" on the back, a moon face, and a marked increase in blood pressure are among the symptoms.) At the Tufts–New England Medical Center, Dr. Anna Binkiewicz, a pediatric endocrinologist, examined a breast-fed four-month-old girl who had been born without complications, weighing about seven pounds at birth, and apparently normal. When the pediatric service saw the child, however, she weighed sixteen pounds, was "balloon-shaped" and had a high level of hormone. The physicians continued to see the child on an outpatient basis, and noticed that she continued to gain weight excessively and grew poorly. In general, they noted that her appearance became even more strongly suggestive of Cushing's syndrome. After she was discharged, the possibility of a connection between the clinical findings and ingestion of alcohol occurred to the doctors.

The Tufts investigators discovered that such was the case. It turned out that though the mother had abstained from drinking during pregnancy, after her child was born she began doing so at the urging of friends who told her it would help milk production. She drank about seven cans of beer a day, as well as "generous amounts of more concentrated alcoholic drinks," and the heavy intake polluted her milk to such an extent that her infant was not only milk-fed but alcohol-fed. "We requested her to stop drinking," said Dr. Binkiewicz, "and she agreed. Breast-feeding was continued. The infant's rate of growth promptly increased and her appearance gradually returned to normal. The mother was pleased with the outcome, but commented that the infant no longer slept as soundly as before."[6]

How long a child whose mother drank during pregnancy will be affected by FAS and events like the case reported by Dr. Binkiewicz depends, of course, on the severity of the symptoms. Mental deficiency shows up in varying degrees, but the lower IQ has been demonstrated in children as old as age 7. Jitteriness, inability to sleep well, and other emotion-based symptoms are observed years after in children who were born with FAS. It is known, too, that the children of alcoholic parents—and especially those whose mothers were alcoholic—often do poorly in school or on the job, withdraw from society, or act out in other ways. Delayed onset of menstruation has also been found in a high percentage of the daughters of mothers who were heavy drinkers during pregnancy. And one study at Georgetown University Hospital found that infants born to mothers who were alcoholics for forty weeks of gestation become true alcoholics themselves and experienced physical withdrawal. "Is this baby a set-up for alcoholism when he or she begins to drink socially?" asked the researcher.

Tracing such behavior directly to the effects of alcohol on fetal life is pure conjecture, but it bears considering along with all of the environmental factors that work on the child of an alcoholic. If one accepts the idea of a chemical basis for emotional illness—we know that drugs can alter moods, and there is strong evidence that schizophrenia is an inherited chemical defect—it is not without reason to assume that alcohol's effects on the brain of the mother, on her moods and behavior, might well be transmitted to the fetus. As Dr. Gellis put it: "Perhaps the tense, hyperexcitable, fearful woman or the opposite type, the depressed, moody, unhappy woman transmits through the placenta substances with which we are familiar, such as adrenaline or glucose in excess or in insufficient amounts, which have their own effect on the fetus. Perhaps we shall someday accept the theory that a pregnant woman who views a defect or upsetting abnormality may indeed produce a fetus with a similar disorder. It is obvious that the pediatric psychiatrist, having stressed the importance of the mother-child relationship during the first few months of the infant's life as critical for the normal future emotional development of the infant, is now indicating that the mother-fetal emotional relationship may be even more critical and that we must somehow convey the importance of regarding happiness as a gay pregnancy."

It's also not known if there is a safe limit of drinking during pregnancy. In the case of the breast-fed Cushing's syndrome infant, the pediatricians said they found no fault with an occasional cocktail or beer taken by the nursing mother. With regard to FAS, most specialists agree that pregnant women ought not to have more than two drinks a day—wine, beer, or cocktails. Again, it depends on how one defines "a drink." If you serve your cocktail in a wine glass and don't measure the liquor, your one drink may be three and your answer to your doctors' questions about your drinking habits won't be all that valid.

Remember that one ounce of 100-proof liquor represents a half-ounce of pure alcohol, and that two cocktails measured with a shot-glass (one ounce) will give you a full ounce of alcohol. A recent study of 9,000 pregnancies in France showed a significant decline in the offspring's birth weight if the mother drank 1.6 ounces of absolute alcohol a day. The critical level seems, then, to be one ounce of pure alcohol—two small drinks—a day. Don't forget, however, that each of us is constructed in ways that may affect how we metabolize alcohol. This means that we each produce different blood levels of the same amounts of the drug, and thus it's not always easy to assess how much a woman should or should not drink during pregnancy. The best route seems to be to do without it if you can. If you can't, then limit your intake. Above all, don't avoid drinking all week just to save up for the weekend so you can have seven drinks at once.

Being careful about drinking is not easy, given the part that alcohol plays in our lives. You might take some comfort in research indicating that pregnant women's desire to drink may be affected by physiological changes. For some pregnant women, alcohol takes on a disagreeable odor and taste, and thus becomes unappealing. "I just don't need what it used to do for me anymore," said a woman who participated in a recent study. Some heavy drinkers, too, have given up the habit on their own after weighing the consequences. "We have been surprised at how readily some alcoholic mothers can stop drinking in the interest of fetal welfare," observes one researcher.

In the latest report on FAS, Dr. David W. Smith, who with Dr. Jones made important original contributions to the recognition and understanding of the disorder, observes:

"In conclusion, studies to date have indicated that in the general population the incidence of FAS may exceed one per 1,000 live births; in the Seattle area, for example, the available data suggests a 0.2 percent incidence of full-blown FAS, with an additional 0.4 percent incidence of newborns with lesser degrees of involvement. Intrauterine exposure to alcohol (which may be by far the number-one fetal teratogen) can thus be regarded as a major public health problem, one that demands a comprehensive program of prevention.

"To prevent FAS, we need to foster in the public the concept of mothering from conception, as opposed to mothering from birth. Every woman of childbearing age should know that the alcohol she drinks during pregnancy is alcohol ingested by her fetus and that, just as she would not want her infant to have alcohol after birth, so she should not want it to have alcohol before birth. The nature and magnitude of the risks involved must be made general public knowledge."[7]

Some physicians have expressed concern that excessive publicity given to FAS might contribute to unnecessary parental guilt and anxiety. This could be the case, and a pregnant woman must remember that the effects of moderate drinking on the fetus are still unclear. Also, two women who consume the same amount of alcohol are not necessarily at the same risk because they may metabolize alcohol in different ways. Their blood alcohol levels, thus, would be different, and their unborn offspring would be at unequal risk.

Unfortunately, the labels on alcohol bottles don't carry warnings about the possible damage to the unborn, or about drinking and taking certain other drugs. Nor do the labels on OTC medicines always include warnings about interactions with alcohol beyond the oblique message that a particular antihistamine causes drowsiness. In the absence of this information, you can do some of the following:

• If you are pregnant, it will pay to be nearly as strict as a Christian Scientist when it comes to drug taking. Take drugs only when absolutely necessary and after discussing each with your doctor.

•   Avoid both cigarettes and alcohol. If you plan to drink, limit your intake.

•   If you must take a drug essential to your health that is known to cause fetal damage, discuss with your physician the possibility of terminating your pregnancy.

•   When discussing the amount you drink, be honest. Define exactly what you mean by "a drink."

•   Report changes in your drinking habits. Some patients who are heavy drinkers, for example, have drug dosages adjusted to the metabolic state of their livers. If they give up drinking, without having the dose adjusted accordingly, the balance could be upset.

•   Don't be reticent about asking your doctor about drug-alcohol reactions. That's what you're paying for. If you are told, "Oh, don't worry about it," press for specific information; if your doctor still cannot satisfy you, contact your pharmacist, the consumer affairs division of your nearest FDA office, your state public health department, or a hospital poison control center.

There should be no excuse for a physician to be uninformed about drug-alcohol interactions. In 1979, HEW Secretary Califano called on the Surgeon General of the U. S. Public Health Service to issue a special advisory to all physicians warning them of the dangers of the combined use of alcohol and certain drugs. Doctors are urged to limit the amount of drug dispensed with each prescription and to monitor prescriptions to patients who may have drinking problems. In addition, information on the dangers of combining alcohol with specific drugs will be published in FDA's *Drug Bulletin,* which is sent to physicians and other health professionals. FDA has also been asked to prepare a list of commonly prescribed drugs that may present health hazards when used with alcohol and for which new warning labels may be needed. Also, the FDA's informative monthly magazine, *FDA Consumer,* carries occasional information about food, drugs, additives, cosmetics, and devices that may pose a danger to health. Subscriptions may be ordered from the Superintendent of Documents, Government Printing Office, Washington, DC 20402, at $12 a year.

•   Read the labels of OTC products and check the package inserts that come with your prescription medications. Your pharmacist, again, is a valuable source of information.

•   When in doubt about whether alcohol will react with the drug you're taking and you've nobody to ask, don't drink.

5

Children
OF ALCOHOLICS

She's only 55, sheet-white hair, looks 70, bloated face—a real mess of a mom.

Miriam, 25, the daughter of an alcoholic
mother

"Drunken women," wrote Aristotle more than 2,000 years ago, "bring forth children like themselves." While the philosopher might have overstated his case, there is a good deal of evidence indicating that the children of alcoholic mothers and/or fathers walk a difficult road. For one thing, there is considerable evidence that the offspring of alcoholics are at increased risk of acquiring a drinking problem. Whether it is an inherited tendency or a childhood spent in an alcoholic environment that destroys the emotional ties between parents and child, alcoholism does run in families. Aware that the mother or father has a drinking problem, or that a grandparent or uncle was destroyed by alcohol, the children are tormented by the obvious question, "Will I become a drunk, too?" Disturbed by the question and often neglected and sometimes abused by the offending parent, children in such an environment are quite often emotionally damaged.

"Children of alcoholics have a high frequency of alcohol misuse, antisocial behavior, neurotic symptoms and psychosomatic complaints," according to the Third Special Report to the U.S. Congress on Alcohol and Health. "A variety of complex factors may interact to produce disturbances in these children, including the personality characteristics of both the alcoholic and nonalcoholic parents, family disorganization, the sociocultural position of the family, and possibly a genetic predisposition to alcoholism."

The report points to a study demonstrating that children of alcoholic fathers were more likely to be admitted to inpatient and outpatient medical facilities for illnesses with no apparent organic cause. Moreover, the effect of the parental alcoholism—in this case the drinking of the father—varied according to the age and sex of the child. Among children who were outpatients and inpatients in mental health facilities, boy and girl outpatients between the ages of 4 and 12 had the same average number of symptoms. After that age, the average number of symptoms in girls increased with age. Among inpatients, the sample included twice as many boys as girls until puberty, when the proportion of girls rose.

"It appears too, that parental alcoholism may be related to delinquency and hyperactivity in children," the report added. "For example, many adolescents treated in a hospital alcoholism unit for drinking problems were referred by courts because of their delinquent behavior, and most had alcoholic fathers. The association between childhood hyperactivity and parental alcoholism also has been supported. One study showed that the parents of hyperactive children had higher adult diagnoses of alcoholism, hysteria, or sociopathy, and that 10 percent of those in the sample were themselves hyperactive as children."

Most studies assessing psychological functioning in children of a sample of alcoholics have shown a high incidence of emotional disturbance, the government report points out. In one, 43 percent of such children aged 10 to 16 were considered very seriously damaged. The children had a difficult time establishing and maintaining friendships, experienced problems in school, and failed to take advantage of recreational programs.

Arlee McGee is a nurse and the chairwoman of a special committee of the New Brunswick (Canada) Alcoholism and Drug Dependency Commission. Children growing up in a home in which alcohol abuse is a way of life, she told a recent meeting, are innocent victims in a number of ways. First, they have to live in an atmosphere of half-truths and white lies. "They learn that parents do not always mean what they say. They may experience verbal and physical abuse; they learn to place no reliance on words, but only on actions. They do not learn the meaning of shared responsibilities. They have few, if any, rights. In fact, they are caught in a constant shift of varying moods and inconsistencies."

Second, there are often double standards, and children are given conflicting guidelines. "They have parents who . . . have weekend drunks, frequently use tranquilizers or other mood-altering substances, have routine cocktail parties—or there may be chronic alcohol use by one or both parents. But these parents preach that the children must abstain or act moderately when it comes to drinking. In other words, 'do as they say, not as they do.' "

The third family situation where children become victims, according to Ms. McGee, is the one in which there is "moralistic preaching of the evils of alcohol" and the atmosphere is so rigid that the children are restricted from learning their own controls or responsibilities. "This foundation fosters rebellious or guilt-ridden adults," she added.

Finally, she said, homes where there is ignorance about drugs and alcohol create an abnormal environment for the child who has to interact in today's society. "Most children recognize the ignorance of parents who do not know the facts on, for example, alcohol or marijuana. Alcohol is our third largest killer. Yet some parents say: 'I'm glad my child only drinks beer and doesn't smoke dope.'"[1]

Caught up in such an environment, children might well become problem drinkers themselves. They might try to outdo the parents by drinking more than they do, in the mistaken notion that this will punish them for their drunkenness. They may simply try to be like them, or, more seriously, try to find the same release and joy that they might equate with their parents' drinking. Or, they may be trying to escape from the grim environment that their parents' drinking behavior has created.

Carla is 30, the daughter of an alcoholic father who worked as a miner in England:

I'm resentful about his drinking, it caused a lot of problems for my mother, who's French. They met after the war. I don't think she really knew what she was getting into, but when he was sober he was fantastic. When he was drunk, he was like a raging bull, an animal. He really was, and he would hit her and the kids, all of us. It was awful.

I'd want to bring kids, friends, home and you just never knew when he'd be sober. There was never any money. We were poor because he drank it all, and I used to go to work at Woolworth's after school to get my mother some money.

I remember it being bad from when I was 3, and it went on forever. It got worse. In the end, after he had thrown my mother down the stairs, I had run away and been found and beaten up by him. It had an unbelievable effect on us all. I threw him out of the house, finally, and my mother eventually got a divorce.

And yet the thing is . . . I would love to see him again. I was in a strange way very close to him. He was an achiever, and the last time I saw him I was 16. I think he gave me drive.

Claudia Black is a clinical social worker who runs CAREUNIT, an alcoholism recovery treatment program at

Parkwood Community Hospital in Canoga Park, California. One of her chief interests is the young children of alcoholics, and she views her work as a way of preventing future psychological problems, including the predisposition of such children to become alcoholic adults or to marry alcoholics. Her contention, however, is that the children from an alcoholic home who exhibit behavioral problems are in the minority, that *all* children with parental alcoholism in their backgrounds, even those who don't act out, are in danger. "I can say with absolute certainty," says Black, "that the 'model' 6-year-old I see in my office today will, without treatment, become the struggling, depressed, soon-to-be-alcoholic 35-year-old I saw yesterday."

Black has discovered three roles that seem to allow children to survive in an alcoholic home: The Responsible One, The Adjuster, and The Placater. The most typical of these roles for the only or the oldest child is that of being overly responsible, not only for himself, but for the other siblings and/or the parents. An example cited by Black is the 10-year-old daughter who takes it upon herself, without telling anyone, to do the daily household chores and attempts to organize the family because the mother is working and the alcoholic father is not. The child extends this sense of responsibility to other areas of her life, excelling in school and learning to manipulate others about her to get done what is necessary. She becomes goal-oriented on a daily basis, learning not to project ahead because her father could interfere, and so her goals become realistic. As she accomplishes these goals, her self-worth develops.

The Adjuster follows directions comfortably and easily and does not feel the pressure of responsibility. One woman Black describes said she felt she had little choice but to adjust, and in the most extreme situations could not follow through with her plans because her parents would move from city to city without notice. Adults who were Adjuster children, Black says, see themselves as flexible and able to adapt to a variety of local situations.

The Placater has a need to smooth over conflicts. Such a child is often extremely sociable, developing the admired quality of helping others to adjust and feel comfortable. Such a child, says Black, often adopts this role to lessen guilt that comes with believing she or he caused the alcohol problem.

Consider the 22-year-old daughter of a male alcoholic who was aware of the tension in the family from the time she was 6. She spent many years trying to help both her parents feel happy, and every time her dad said, "Let's go for a ride," she would go. Now, in her adulthood, she is aware that the ride always meant stopping at local taverns. "She combined the placating and responsible roles," says Black, "additionally doing a great amount of housework to please the mother, who worked because dad did not work. For hours at a time, she would wait on and listen to dad's buddies as they drank and talked. She said she did not understand what was happening in the home, but she knew people hurt, and she would do whatever she could to please them, thinking it would take away the pain. Strengths developed out of this role. She felt she was popular and got many strokes for helping others, being sensitive to their feelings, and listening well."[2]

Cornelia Wallace is the former First Lady of Alabama, ex-wife of George Wallace. Her mother is Ruby Folsom Austin, whom we met earlier:

[A] political family's no exception. Everybody's got some kind of problem in their family and when you're in politics you just dread to have these things become public because you think they're goin' to hurt you or cost you a few votes or whatever. But the truth is that people today really appreciate you more for your honesty—you know, they've been deceived so much.

I didn't want to tell people that my mother had this kind of addiction to alcohol because I didn't want to hurt her by talkin' about her or even havin' it known, because it is painful for her. . . . But by the same token, it is a real part of our life, and havin' to try to keep it a secret and worryin' about it, people knowin' about it, was a terrific strain. . . .

Mothers tend to give children a lot of emotional support and I think that you go to your mother for that. My mother's alcohol problem was bad enough that before I got married, Governor Wallace and I tried twice to get her into treatment. And she didn't go. Her drinking was at the stage where I had stopped all her in-coming calls. I would not accept calls for her.

My brother and George both, we had a family meeting about this . . . and they said, "Ruby, don't you think you can stop drinkin' all by yourself?" Well, see, I knew that she didn't have any control over it, over alcohol; I knew she wasn't doin' that by choice. . . . She was addicted and she was helpless, she couldn't do it by herself, why, I knew she couldn't. . . . I knew my mother was a tough case, she's just tough. I know the lady. I don't know much about alcoholism, but I know this lady. . . .

The family concept of that treatment at the institute in Palm Beach is what really appealed to me, and it was the only reason that I encouraged her. I was aware that I had been involved, and that it had all affected me. . . . I had always rescued her from her alcoholic crises and I knew that I shouldn't do that. . . . But I did it.

I don't drink. . . . Public image? I thought my public image was good . . . [the fact that my mother drank] didn't keep George from marryin' me, and he knew all about it then. He knew that my mother had a problem . . . and he knew that if I were the First Lady of Alabama that there would be a lot of attention brought to me and my family and my mother.

It wasn't her drinkin' that made the difference in my own campaign for governor, it was the lack of money. Her problem with alcohol was insignificant to me except that I could never depend on her, she was never available. . . .

My mother's havin' a drinkin' problem made me do more things, made me more independent because I didn't sit around waitin' for my mother to do it for me. I knew that if it got done, I had to do it for myself, and I think I'm a more capable person because of it. By the time I was 15, 16, I was a whole lot more responsible. If she had one drink too many, I'd say that was the time to go home. I was role substituting with her. . . .

Her bein' public gives her an image of sobriety that's important to her. . . . She's made a change. I can see it happen to her. What made me feel so good was that I had been carryin' this tension around forever:

Mother havin' this drinking problem and not wantin' to hurt her by ever sayin' anything public on it and so afraid the press was goin' to nail it on me. I felt so released when she didn't have anything to hide anymore. . . . It's really a good feeling.[3]

Cornelia Wallace is a survivor. It's been hard, but she has dealt with her mother's problem and may even credit some of her drive and self-sufficiency to a childhood of necessary strength. But there are negative consequences, too, for some of these bright, responsible, adapting, and sociable "alcoholic offspring." As they reach their late teens and early twenties, says Black, they are often very aware of their strengths, aware that friends and relatives are pleased that they have done so well, despite the horrible homelife in which they were reared. As a consequence, they do not change roles when they leave the alcoholic environment. But eventually they realize that their old methods of coping are no longer effective in bringing meaning to life.

"It is at this time," Black believes, "that the effects of living in the alcoholic home begin to show. These adults often find themselves depressed, and they do not understand why; life seems to lack meaning. They feel a loneliness, though many are not alone. Many find great difficulty in maintaining intimate relationships. And many become alcoholics and/or marry alcoholics."

Many of the children also learned it was not acceptable for them to show anger or sadness, that it did no good to feel, that no one was there to comfort them, that they were ignored when they needed to talk about important things. This can and does affect later life. One 25-year-old woman, the daughter of a male alcoholic, remained unaware of the problems that had set in until she walked out of a 5-year-old marriage, one in which she never argued and which was marked by her depression. It took several months of therapy to get her to acknowledge her fear of her anger and her own anger, and to begin working on accepting that feeling in herself and in others. Another woman, who had carried her role as placater into adulthood, had this to say: "After I raised my kids and only had my husband to please, it seemed life had little meaning, and before long I was here in the hospital for alcoholism."

Gretchen is 25, a retail clothes buyer in a Seattle department store, the daughter of an alcoholic mother:

When I was a kid, going through all this with my mother, I thought all mothers were like that. Honestly, I did not know that my house was different, that your mother was not supposed to smack you around all the time. I thought that everyone's family had scenes if they had kids because the kids were rebellious, and it never ever occurred to me that my mother had a drinking problem. . . .

I read more and more and finally realized what was going on with her. She was completely protected at home by my father, and my mother's mother used to drink a lot and make scenes and call and all, and my mother would say, "If I get like that, tell me." Now if I say to her, "Hey, you're just like your mother, you're doing the same thing all over again," she'll say, "No, no, no, that's not true." And my father says . . . nothing. . . . If you tell her about the drinking, it's like you've spoken to her in Russian. She'll say, "Don't get on me like that, leave me alone, I've done my job as a mother, I'm happy." She'll tell you she's not an alcoholic because she doesn't drink in the morning and doesn't get hangovers. . . .

Well, she doesn't ever have a drink before 5:00, not even on a Saturday or Sunday. She might have a gin and tonic before noon but that's it. On a weekend, usually, if there are people. But at 5:00, the gun goes off and she just drinks. Straight bourbon. And she'll do a quart between 5:00 and 7:00.

You sit down at the table and she's like a raving lunatic at the [other] end . . . then she usually passes out, wakes up a couple hours later, and wants to know where the party is. And Dad is at the other end of the table. . . .

Everybody loves her because she's a really wonderful lady, very gregarious. It's pretty much a situation where the people who come by the house know she's like this and pretty much ignore her and her problem

. . . even though she's at the end of the table making no sense at all and carrying on. Everyone fights over who's going to sit next to her, and nobody wants to because if you're that person she's got you, your ear's bent off. . . .

This has been going on as long as I can remember, maybe fifteen years. Ever since we were little kids there were drunken parties, and it was an accepted thing. I was the only kid who could fall asleep to fifteen people singing in the living room. . . .

Every night it's the same thing with her and when she's done she drinks coffee and hides in that. She's been sick, too, liver trouble, in the hospital for six months at a stretch, had something done to her stomach once, I think. They'd tell her, "No more drink," and that'd last two, three weeks. And now it's her gall bladder and blood pressure that's outrageously high. She's also extremely overweight, consumes massive amounts of sweets—I've seen her go through a whole pie. She does that after she passes out, gets hungry and has to eat a whole bunch of pie.

It's just the two of them at home now, Mother and Dad; the kids, including me, have long gone. He just doesn't argue with her about it any more, and I doubt he ever did. It's easier that way for him, I suppose. They have dinner—he does, anyway—and she goes to bed eventually and he gets his work done. He spends a lot of time just trying to heal things, I think, because she becomes just bitter and hostile after she's been drinking.

I think my mother hates me a lot. And you know, it only comes out when she's smashed. It's so weird, schizophrenic even. If someone is sitting there next to her she will go on about how wonderful I am and how successful I am and how terrific it is to have a daughter doing this big buying thing. Then later she'll turn around and grab hold of my arm and say, "What the hell's the matter with you, you're going straight down hill. You're not married, can't keep a guy, screwing around." She's done it the right way, she'll tell me, and why can't I do that, too?

I think she's bored and she's jealous and she's angry and she's miserable and she's drunk; and maybe to have me, this young woman, coming into the house doing everything, a lot of the housework and stuff, makes her feel replaced, and that's what it's all about. She has told people, I know, that she's had a wonderful thing going with Dad and didn't want me to ruin it. I'm sure she feels very threatened by the close relationship I have with Dad. She has walked around the house saying,

"Somebody else is taking my place." But what the hell, you can't trust her to cook, right? She can't clean the place. She can't change the sheets.

She still treats me worse than she treats the other kids. She calls me a slut, a whore, when are you going to settle down, all that. But when she's in trouble, I'm the one she calls. I think she hates me so much because she's so vulnerable to me. See, I know her so well, I'm the one who helped her and she throws that back by not liking me. I know her secrets. She has dreams, she tells me, that she's me. She really does. Young and running around, like me. I wish she could have done all the things she thinks I'm doing, or have done, and she's pissed that liberation didn't happen for her. But the same time, she doesn't have enough balls to turn around and say, "I can do it today. . . ."

She ought to get a job. She's terrific with people when she's sober. I say, "Why don't you get a job selling real estate, or help set up a community center?" She has a degree in art, but she never did a thing with it. A bookstore maybe. But no. She plays mah-jong with her friends and watches TV.

I'm embarrassed a lot by her. When I take somebody home now, it's rare. I used to say, while I was in college, to a guy, "Look, before you meet my mother there's something you should know: She drinks a lot." Now I tell them she's an alcoholic and she will lose her cookies around 6:00, so don't pay any attention to her. You take a guy home for the first time, and you like him, and you figure he ought to like your mom and father. And then at 6:00 your mom starts to go down the tubes. She starts pulling this guy's shirt off and asks him how much money he makes and are his intentions honorable, does he sleep with me. I just can't take that anymore. . . .

It's not what mothers are supposed to be. When she's sober she wants to know why I don't bring the guys around anymore, and when she visits my apartment the phone'll ring and she'll say, "When am I going to meet some of these fellows?" And I say, "You'll meet them the day I marry one of them."

My father doesn't get too involved because, I think, it's part of his makeup. In his home when he was a kid, you never spoke up or yelled back. He doesn't really seem to understand my mother's anger or her emotions. I know he would never leave her or divorce her. But he has told me that if he had it to do over again he would never have gotten married. . . . I don't want to sell my mother short because she has been *a good lady in a lot of respects, but he does deserve a nice lady on his arm. . . .*

I still have a traditional image of a mother who is kind and loving and not cold, abrasive, and who can't go to your high school graduation because she's smashed out of her gourd. . . .

I do call her regularly because I feel if I don't hear from her for a while something's happened, she's killed herself. Nobody else seems to bother with her. My brothers avoid her like the plague. They don't discuss her situation, have no patience with her at all, and whenever I raise the necessity for getting her some help they'll just say, "No, forget it, it's too late."

But you know, if it were Dad out drunk and screwing up I know they'd be banging on the door of wherever he was to get him out and straightened. They've done it for other male relatives who've had problems—but Mother, they write her off.

John is 25, a freelance writer living in Palo Alto, California. His mother is a recovered alcoholic, and unlike Gretchen, he has come to terms with his anger and hostility over his mother's problem. Yet the experience has left other scars: John recognizes in himself addictive tendencies similar to his mother's. And it bothers him:

I think a lot now about my mother's alcoholism, her brother's alcoholism, alcoholism on my father's side. I do have this great fear of becoming like them. It's not illogical, given what I've learned about the inherited factors.

I do drink much less than I did in college, when it was ten, twelve beers. And there was then, and there is, I'm sorry to admit, a love for drinking on my part. Maybe this gene pool is really strong for us. We used to say, my brother and I, that we couldn't ever imagine our uncle Joe without that smell of beer on his breath. But with my mother, she didn't really drink a lot at all, really couldn't handle her alcohol. . . . We used to, as a defense, sort of imitate her. She had a certain way she would talk when she drank. Her voice would become, well, bleary. . . and she'd have this sort of sick smile. So my sister and I would imitate this, making the smile or copying the voice. . . .

It's funny, but for the past couple of years, since my sophomore year at college, I've had a fairly steady and relatively heavy marijuana habit, and there's no question in my mind that I've done that so I wouldn't drink. I've thought that it was the lesser of two evils, that is it's not . . . indigenous to my life like alcohol is. I very rarely drink hard liquor, and maybe this is all a delusion, but after I drink I feel really bad the next day. I do see the marijuana as a manifestation of an addictive personality, the same kind of personality that makes me want to read more. I've got to keep learning more and more. I live with people who also smoke, and I think that has a lot to do with it, too.

You know, I don't buy it, not in the last five years. And I've noticed that I sometimes exhibit the same traits as a drinker. Like I'll sneak it from my roommates without asking, and I'll be around people who I know will buy it or bring it to a party, or I'll think about having a joint while I'm writing, looking forward to it when I get home. The whole idea of having to hide it anyway because it's illegal gives it that . . . surreptitious quality . . . that I know goes with problem drinking. I just hope there'll come a day when I won't want either.

Insofar as Mother's drinking is concerned, for all of us it was just the latest thing. She had all kinds of vague pains, shock treatments, psychiatric counseling, physical and emotional problems, and to me the alcoholism was, in a funny way, almost a relief because it was something you could put your finger on.

In her case, it developed into a sort of life-saving thing, . . . maybe a better way to put it is a way of life—because she got involved with AA, and she found a kind of identity that she had been lacking. Ever since then she's been really a fairly solid individual. You know, she was really down and out, and she did pick herself up. I think that's had a very human effect on all of us. That she could do it. She was so helpless. I'm really quite proud of the lady, not angry or hostile over it all.

My sister was angry. My mother wasn't being a mother to her, and I can understand that. She's younger and has different needs, and she ended up being the mother herself at a very early age. But maybe I guess I never really believed my mother was an alcoholic until she said she was. I probably did a lot of denying about that and maybe that's why I didn't feel angry. But even later, though, when it all became clearer what her problem was, I still did not feel judgmental or angry. I realized, look, this is a middle-aged widow woman, a house and kids to take care of, a woman who started drinking only in later years right after my dad died. And I can understand that totally. It was something in her that was building up. She got in with some friends who drank and I think, on top of everything else, that had something to do with it all. I've read since that sometimes an inherited weakness can interact with environmental events, and that combination can lead to alcoholism. And my mother certainly had both.

It could happen to me. After all, drinking is very much a part of my family's history.

I did get exasperated on occasion with her, but ashamed of her, never. I remember one time punching in a door when she was acting stupid after drinking, and I suppose I did test her on occasion. Like once I took her to dinner and ordered a beer, and she looked at me and said, "You know you shouldn't have done that." I think I did know what I was doing when I ordered it, and I said, "I'll cancel it," but she said, "No." It was probably dumb, and I didn't do it again.

I'm not the oldest in the family, but in recent years I have taken on a lot more responsibility at home. I've looked after my sister's problems a lot more than the others have and maybe this comes from the time my dad was sick for so long at home.

I like to think that, just as the whole experience has helped my mother find herself, in a lot of ways . . . it helped get us closer and it helped me in other ways, too. It's made me think a lot about myself, my goals and all. I guess I don't want to screw up like that, I don't want to let anything get in the way of my writing. And I see guys all around me, friends of mine on the newspapers in New York, strung out on booze. It's not just the old guys, either. There's a lot of burned-out cases on papers, and I don't want to wind up on some nightside copy desk, 4:00 p.m. to 1:00 in the morning, playing Scrabble and hanging paragraph marks on copy that I should be writing.

There may also be something very positive in being an addictive personality. You can become so absorbed in your projects, something as simple as reading a book. I go at it til I finish. And writing. I'll stick to a project for a magazine, for example, without letting anything get in the way. Some people translate that into booze, and I've done it with grass. I just hope it'll stay channelled in the right direction. Thinking of my mother's drinking always puts me back on the track.

6

Helping
THE
ALCOHOLIC

When I go looking for a job or start getting to know someone, I tell them I'm a recovered alcoholic. I tell people because I don't want to deny any part of me. Being alcoholic is part of the total human being I am.

Elaine, 39, a receptionist who had help

The stigma that is still attached to alcoholism and the pessimism that many still feel about its treatment stem, in part at least, from the centuries-old idea that moral degeneracy is at the disorder's core. In fact, compulsive drinking that impairs a person's social functioning, family relationships, and bodily health—in combination or singly—was defined by the AMA as an illness less than twenty-five years ago. The widespread custom of assigning the problem to the criminal justice system and putting drunks in jail or mental institutions continued into the early 1970s. At that time, the Uniform Alcoholism and Intoxication Treatment Act came into being and is being adopted and modified by many states. It mandates the establishment of detoxification and acute care services for intoxicated individuals and removes them from the criminal justice system.

Another program that reinforces alcoholism as a physical handicap rather than a punishable offense is one funded by the U.S. Department of Transportation to help persons convicted of drunken driving receive treatment. By agreement with the courts in a growing number of cities, these people have a choice to either enter treatment or have their licenses suspended. Although there is great controversy over this form of involuntary treatment, those professionals working with the program are supportive and find that in many cases, treatment has given the participants a new lease on life.

Until very recently, hospital treatment aimed at helping alcoholics to remain sober was available only to those wealthy enough to afford it. However, though federal, state, and local government funds constitute a significant proportion of the resources for alcoholism treatment at the present time, there has been an impressive increase in the number of third-party reimbursements from private insurance carriers. For instance, comprehensive alcoholism benefits are being offered by individual Blue Cross plans. Some offer alcoholism treatment in special inpatient centers and others provide innovative outpatient care. Blue Cross coverage for the United Auto Workers union includes both residential and outpatient treatment.

State legislatures are concerned about the availability of insurance for alcoholism treatment, and several states have enacted legislation mandating either that alcoholism coverage be provided or that it be available as an option.

However, although recognized as a physical handicap, alcoholism is not curable, despite the allusion to cure that the words disease, disorder, and illness conjure. A handicap is probably the best way to define problem drinking; not only is it more accurate than disease, but its connotation of shortcoming, of impediment, implies that the person can be helped to function nearly as well as those who are not so hindered. Alcoholism is like that—recognizable and treatable, but incurable.

There is, of course, no single treatment because there is no single cause. Alcoholism has its roots in the unique complexity of each individual. Just as there are over 100 different kinds of cancer that have a variety of causes and, therefore, specific treatments, so, too, are there different alcoholisms that require individual approaches.

We have presented theories about the reasons for women's drinking behavior, and many of them, as we have seen, seem contradictory. The assumptions that have been made quite often do not apply in all cases. Moreover, the research done on women and alcohol use and abuse is uncoordinated, often poorly constructed, sometimes an afterthought. Fortunately, interest in women and alcohol has increased over the last ten years, and with that interest there is hope that better treatment for women with drinking problems—something that male alcoholics have been able to obtain more easily—will follow.

Therapeutic approaches for the female alcoholic—indeed, therapy for women, in general—have been accused of having a male orientation that reinforces the devaluation of women. Women, as we have said, far outdistance men in their utilization of both medical and psychological services. Women not uncommonly enter therapy with tremendous feelings of inadequacy and self-hatred, with self-destructive thoughts and sometimes a history of threatening actions. It is reported that the number of suicide attempts is much higher among women than men, probably because men more often turn their anger toward others. Women are guilt-ridden and blame themselves for their unhappiness; thus they often turn their resentment against themselves. They see themselves as failures, then people around them tend to see them as failures. The result is depression, anxiety, and self-loathing.

And coupled with the problems a woman's special needs

present, the fact that an overwhelming majority of therapists are male and white—90 percent of practicing psychiatrists and 67 percent of clinical psychologists—leaves no question that alternative approaches to therapy for women are essential.

"Because so many therapists have not questioned the influence of stereotypes and psychological theories on therapy for women, they often do not understand fully what role a woman's environment plays in creating or intensifying problems," say Susan S. Friedman and her coauthors in their recent book, *A Woman's Guide to Therapy*. "Like women themselves, therapists tend to see problems as unique, as arising out of personal failures to cope with the world. They are likely to try to help women *adjust* to this environment rather than helping them *change* their situations. In seeking to free women from their problems and push them in the direction of individual fulfillment, therapists are all too likely to urge a discretion consistent with their own notion of what fulfillment means for a woman."

Attempts are being made at a variety of levels to make therapy sensitive to women's issues and beneficial to women's search for strength in a hostile society. Among these is a new school that has emerged from a decade of scholarship and political organization: feminist therapy. It takes the perspectives of feminism and applies them to the therapeutic situation—that is, to both the content and process of therapy. Feminist scholars Diane Kravetz and Jeanne Marecek have described the goals of feminist therapy as "helping women to discover their personal strengths, to achieve a sense of independence, to view themselves as equals in interpersonal relationships, and to respect and trust themselves and other women."[1]

The word "feminist" sometimes has negative connotations, however, and may frighten many women away from such treatment. One feminist therapist had this to say: "Demystify the word 'feminist' for your readers. Some women are afraid that a feminist therapist will be hard, strident, and dogmatic and want her clients to become that way. All the false stereotypes of 'feminists' in general have been just as falsely applied to feminist therapists. A feminist therapist is not an ogre who hates men and forces women to abandon marriage. The label is much more likely to mean that she will be open to explore with women their urge to develop an identity that does not sacrifice its autonomy to the wishes and demands of men and children."

It is heartening to note that these advances in women's therapy have carried over to the recently established women's alcoholism treatment centers. It is not surprising that until recently alcohol treatment programs were ill equipped to deal with women alcoholics. Historically, women have received low-priority attention in nontraditional areas, thereby establishing a cultural protective device for women who are problem drinkers. As noted in previous chapters, families and medical professionals frequently have tended to disguise female alcoholism under less embarrassing diagnoses, effectively eliminating treatment.

Even today, physicians are still reluctant to manage female alcoholic patients. Because the hand that rocks the cradle is not *supposed* to be shaky from liquor, all of the things about alcoholic males that turn physicians off—their seemingly hopeless situation, their negligence about paying bills, their denials—seem somehow worse in women. Many physicians are also concerned that they may have to bear full responsibility for treating an alcoholic woman because of society's attitude of denying the problem, which has contributed to the relative scarcity of adequate treatment programs. The result is often no treatment—or anti-anxiety drugs.

Another barrier to treatment is the well-documented fact that women, who spend more time at home than men do, tend to drink at home alone and, therefore, less visibly. This means that a woman often doesn't get into treatment until she hits the bottom, a situation that might have been prevented if someone—family, friends, an alert and caring doctor, the problem drinker herself—had intervened earlier.

Encouraging signs for women's treatment do exist, however. More women are entering treatment, and initial studies of post-treatment behavioral changes indicate positive prognoses in many cases. Many therapy programs are co-educational. The problem with some of these is that females in mixed-group programs tend to relate better to one another, thus depriving the woman problem drinker of the comradeship of, and acceptance by, men, which is so important. But women's treatment groups are becoming more numerous: Both patients and health professionals have begun to realize that the woman drinker's needs are unique.

One model program that attempts to address the specific treatment needs of alcoholic women is in the Boston area, known as The Women's Alcoholism Program of CASPAR (Cambridge and Somerville Program for Alcoholism Rehabilitation). One of seven programs initially funded in 1975 by the NIAAA, it now offers comprehensive services to alcoholic women and their families and friends, and develops educational training programs for other community workers. A woman who wishes to enter the program must be the mother of at least one pre-school or school-aged child and she must have abstained from all liquor for three days. Upon acceptance, she is provided with an individual counselor who meets with her at least once a week.

The staff, directed by Norma Finkelstein, is especially sensitive to the shame and guilt they know is more internalized in women. They also know, only too well, that because women drunks didn't hang around street corners, people figured they didn't exist. Take Nancy, a heavy drinker. Some years ago when she turned yellow, her doctor attributed it to a vitamin deficiency. When her kidneys stopped working, he suggested she might have a liver problem. It wasn't until three days before she died that the doctor realized his patient had cirrhosis, the drinker's disease.

Finkelstein said that often, by the time a woman comes to

the program for help, she's lost her children to a relative or to state care. But "taking the children out of the home and placing them in a foster home is not always the answer, either," says Dr. Ruth Sanchez-Dirks, Special Assistant to the Director of the NIAAA. The children of alcoholic parents feel responsible for the behavior of their parents and often take on the role of parents in the family system. Therefore, she says, "removal of the children from the home increases the guilt, the feeling that they have done something wrong, or have failed their parents. If the parents do not visit their children in a foster home, feelings of failure are intensified. Much work needs to be done both with the parents and the children so that children can return to the parental home. Many times, once children are in protective custody, agencies seem to forget that their mission is not only to protect the children but to return them to their parents as well. This is the very thing that alcoholic mothers fear and cite as a deterrent to coming for treatment."[2]

The fact that the woman is usually directly responsible for her children has far-reaching implications for the treatment plan of the woman alcoholic. Current treatment for all alcoholics usually includes treating the family as well, but when a woman has bowed down to booze, keeping her family intact is a real challenge. Her long-suffering husband soon throws in the towel because this woman who bears his name and his children has shamed them all. And husbands don't generally stay around as long as wives do if the situation were reversed.

CASPAR also makes use of a home in Cambridge as a day treatment center for alcoholic mothers with young children. Nonresidential, it focuses on helping the women develop skills that will help her keep her family together. Included in a typical four-days-per-week schedule are group sessions addressing such topics as their alcoholism experience, nutrition, exercise, personal growth, women's issues, alcoholism education, and survival skills. Also included is time for relaxation, a mothers' group, and a regularly scheduled Alcoholics Anonymous meeting, as well as another speaker's meeting. Leisure time specialists are brought in, because this is an especially vulnerable area for women alcoholics attempting to recover. At the end of the day, on Friday, there is a process group, which encourages the participants to discuss what they have done the previous week and what their weekend plans are. Most of these women are single parents and they are encouraged to keep in touch with one another.

The hope offered to these women and their children is a far cry from the medieval approaches of abandonment and confinement to a mental institution or jail, which were the only alternatives open to women with alcohol-related problems until only a few short years ago. The need for such programs is unquestionably great and it is expected that many more will be established across the nation.

Another special program for women provided by this same group is a half-way house offering residential care to sober alcoholic women. Womanplace is a fifteen-bed AA-oriented half-way house with a program that includes individual and group counseling, alcohol education, vocational guidance, family counseling, and a variety of other services that address the special circumstances of the alcoholic woman. The staff is composed, for the most part, of reformed alcoholic women who show a very real commitment to the residents. Because of the multiple problems women have in trying to maintain sobriety, the program is highly structured. After about three months, there is a gradual loosening up, and more individual responsibility is undertaken by the self-referred women.

Priority for placement is given to women who live in the Cambridge/Somerville area, women known to the alcoholism program, and women in detoxification. There is always a waiting list, since there are, unfortunately, too few homes such as this for women preparing to re-enter community life. The average stay at Womanplace is seven to ten months. During this time, residents are encouraged to take holiday weekends, and to use outside support, such as AA, family, and friends, whenever possible to ease the transition to the next step beyond the half-way house. The women in the program range in age from 18 to 63.

The program encourages the women to express anger and to get in touch with their feelings. It is here and now that they must learn to live with a new set of survival skills. Especially challenging to counselors is that these women, when sober, have a very low energy level and they are not too motivated at the beginning of sobriety. Also, physical withdrawal sometimes takes longer because the woman has hidden her drinking—she has gone so far down in her self-degradation that it takes longer for her to get back.

As we noted earlier, many rehabilitated women find that, by the time they have acknowledged their need for treatment, they have lost their husbands as well as their children. Statistics from a federally sponsored study of women and alcohol points out that for every ten wives who see an alcoholic husband through, only one husband remains with an alcoholic wife. No one can safely say whether this loss is beneficial, but if a woman has been superdependent on her husband, this dependency may be replaced with a determination to remain sober. Maintaining that balance of independence and sobriety for long periods of time is the mark of real change in her life.

However, this same report revealed that single women who are alcoholics usually have more difficulties in recovering than do married women. "American society has no clearly defined role for the unattached woman," the report said. "This may make it very difficult for a single woman to find the social acceptance and self-acceptance that is necessary for recovery."

Alcoholism has not spared women in any race, economic background, or profession, the report added. Sensitive to this fact, the Women's Alcoholism Program of CASPAR has begun to look at the needs of special cultural and ethnic groups of women. One such group, lesbian alcoholics, is receiving a good deal of attention because of the efforts of a number of women who are determined to help society understand their special problems. Nancy T. is one such woman. At a recent symposium at Rutgers University, she told of the lesbian alcoholic's quadruple alienation from the society in which she lives: "She is alienated from the world simply in being alcoholic. Second, she is alienated in being a woman; third, in being homosexual; and fourth, in being female in a gay subculture largely dominated by male interests, activities, and socializing patterns."[3]

Limited research points to high incidence of alcoholism in the gay community. Researcher Lillene Fifield and her associates found a 32-percent incidence; the Reverend Joan Johnson, in her work sponsored by the Universal Fellowship of Metropolitan Community Churches, found up to 75-percent incidence; the research of Thomas O. Ziebold indicates that lesbians have ten times the incidence of alcoholism that heterosexual women have. Nancy T. feels that it may be comparable to those of other minority groups. She told the Rutgers group that the reasons for the higher-than-average incidence of alcoholism in homosexuals are many and complex, but primarily boil down to two factors: the gay bar as the primary social outlet and personal and community alienation.

The Alcoholism Center for Women, a treatment facility in Los Angeles that specializes in services to lesbians, finds that the problems of the lesbian alcoholic are similar to those of nongay women, but are exacerbated by society's prejudices, stereotypes, misunderstandings, and hostilities toward lesbians. "The lives of many gay women are characterized by fragmentation, compartmentalization, isolation, and desperation. A common strain running through these women's experiences is self-doubt, low self-esteem, and feelings of inadequacy."

The Center says that "effective treatment processes must begin with a staff which is not only sensitive and aware, but has a positive understanding of lesbian behaviors, attitudes, and life-styles. The creation of an environment of caring [and] supportive safety is especially crucial to effective treatment of lesbian alcoholics, since much of their lives have been spent hiding an important part of themselves."

A look at a lesbian alcoholic's experience and need for treatment may help us understand what happens when awareness of and sensitivity to her special problems are lacking:

I began to seek psychiatric help when the woman I lived with for years committed suicide. I was drinking heavily, couldn't accept her death, and had no idea how to continue my life. When the anxiety became unbearable I checked into a hospital. The interviewing doctor told me they would be able to help me. Oblivious to the fact that I managed to get drunk every day for fifteen months in the hospital, they began to assault my lesbianism: Sometimes they assigned me an aide to follow me around the ward; they threw me into 'preventative' seclusion; they investigated all my relationships with the other women patients, and on occasion threatened to interrupt friendships with massive doses of tranquilizers.

Doctors have told me I was utterly dependent (love women), had anxiety neuroses (alcohol withdrawal), was borderline schizophrenic (failed to conform to their idea of what a woman's life should be), and had a poor prognosis (I believed in myself more than in their theories about me).

In the few years following, things got worse: The drinking that threatened my life wasn't interesting to them. When I was close to dying, a clinic slip read, 'Patient says she is alcoholic.' But all the doctors were willing to ship me away permanently to the back wards of state hospitals, not because I was harming myself (drinking is just a symptom, they said), but because I lived wrongly. I could feel their need to punish me for not giving in to their opinions of what was wrong with my life—that is, I defended lesbianism as one of the more positive and beautiful aspects of my life. Yet they were so into forcing my life to conform to their theories that while I was literally dying of alcoholism they wanted to know what my lover and I did in bed.

Before any further discussion of the specific treatment needs of alcoholic women, some digression to the goals of treatment programs in general—and to their major approaches—might be helpful. First off, you should be fully aware that the aim of most programs is total and permanent abstinence. Realization of such a goal, however, is not an easy task, as many alcoholics will tell you. Some specialists maintain that only about 20 percent of all treated patients are able to remain abstinent for more than three years, others place the figure higher. There are also those who argue that some alcoholics can drink moderately, that therapy in such individuals is still helpful even though it doesn't lead to abstinence, and that what is important is the relative quality of the life the individual lives. It is not our purpose to campaign for one or the other of these views, but to acknowledge that there are, despite the popular view, two sides to the question, and to present both.

Among those who took the view that some alcoholics can return to normal drinking was a group from the University of Cincinnati College of Medicine and the Alcoholism Clinic of the Cincinnati Health Department. In 1965, they reported that of thirty-two ex-alcoholics studied at the clinic, at least a year after treatment, eleven were totally abstinent, ten were compulsive drinkers, and eleven more were classified as normal drinkers. The researchers suggested that some people can be alcoholic for reasons that can be changed with treatment. They also pointed out that abstinence in itself does not necessarily mean overall improvement in a patient because neuroses or other difficulties may remain even though the drinker has quit. Ten years later, the Rand Corporation released an equally controversial report suggesting that some alcoholics can return to normal drinking after treatment with no more danger than teetotalers. The report based its findings on data collected from several treatment programs sponsored by the NIAAA. In all fairness, it must be pointed out that the authors of the report cautioned against the assumption that it would be safe for all alcoholics to resume drinking. There was no way, they said, to tell the difference between those who can safely drink again and those who cannot.

Numerous studies have refuted those who claim that a return to moderate drinking—the term used is "controlled drinking"—is possible for alcoholics. Dr. Ernest Noble, current director of the NIAAA, has warned, in fact, that abstinence must continue as the appropriate goal in the treatment of alcoholism. It would be unwise, he says, for a recovered alcoholic to even try to experiment with controlled drinking.

Most treatment programs, as we have said, tend to agree. In Topeka, Kansas, the Alcoholism Recovery Program of the Menninger Foundation is a good example. One of the program's basic rules is that if a patient continues to drink while in the program, treatment is terminated. "Our policy is that drinking is incompatible with treatment goals," says Dr. John Connelly, the director. "But if a patient slips once that doesn't mean he's automatically discharged. It does mean, however, that his lapse is going to be a real treatment issue. If it happens a second time, we'd have to take a serious look at how committed he is to change."

As for controlled drinking, Connelly is against it. The alcoholic, he believes, pays a heavy price for such a move and it is often tried at the expense of self-development and growth. "Although there are some programs that claim to teach alcoholics to drink moderately, the more the person has abused alcohol in the past, the higher the risk of abusing it again. Any group study of alcoholics will report some small percentage of people who have gone back to moderate drinking, but these people don't drink moderately in the way a nonalcoholic would. They have to exercise rigid control on the boundaries of their drinking and they do not drink without guilt or tension."[4]

Again, if a woman lapses temporarily during her treatment, this should not be taken to mean failure. "The goal of every program," says the AMA, "should be to help the alcohol-dependent patient learn to deal effectively with life problems without using the drug and to adapt to his or her environment in a reasonably mature manner. As in many other diseases, relapses may take place but must never be thought to indicate that recovery is beyond reach. Any improvement is positive and should be recognized and encouraged as a prelude to recovery."

Treatment of the female alcoholic may be handled by medical and nonmedical specialists. Behavioral therapy, aversion techniques, supportive psychotherapy, peer counseling, drug treatment, and group therapy are all employed on either an outpatient or in-residence basis. Many of the programs require that the patient mingle in the community and seek employment to help in the rehabilitation process. Families are involved in the treatment, and some programs provide day care facilities.

This last is most important if an alcoholic woman whose husband has walked out has children to care for. "Even when the husband remains in the home, if he is employed, what frees the wife to participate in rehabilitation activities during his working hours?" was a question asked at a recent research conference of the Association for Women in Psychology. "Too often, unfortunately, for both the woman and her children, these questions remain unanswered. And often the woman who admits to being alcoholic and seeks treatment runs the risk of having her children removed from her by legal means. This often exacerbates the alcoholism problem by introducing the despair of enforced separation with no provision made for dealing with the condition that precipitated the removal. This fear of legal retribution forces many women to continue to hide the alcoholism and try to cope."

The Menninger Foundation's recovery program, which is now seeing an increasing number of women patients, is an example of a facility that combines group therapy, research, and follow-up. The program is six to eight weeks long for the inpatient phase, and a total of two years is allowed for extensive follow-up treatment and research. Admission is voluntary, although nearly all the patients enter under a certain amount of pressure from close friends, relatives, or employers.

Groups are common, both single-sex and mixed, and are usually confrontation-oriented—that is, the reality of drinking is the chief concern, and each member's rationalization system is a target for group criticism. Once sobriety is achieved, the members can move on to other issues of loneliness, poor interpersonal relationships, and neurotic behavior. Any loss of sobriety by one member of the group turns it back to its first order of business.

There is a good deal of dispute over whether women do better in mixed groups or in settings that are exclusively female, where they can find more support and empathy. While no one is really certain whether women fare better with other women, there seems to be little doubt that women and men behave differently in treatment. Dr. Stephanie Brown, associate director of the Stanford Medical Center Alcohol Clinic, tells of the guilt of the alcoholic woman and of how she feels "less than normal," approaching life ready to blame herself for any difficulties. Women, she says, are less defensive than men, and wish to increase independent and assertive behavior. Men, expressing an opposite ideal, would decrease their autonomy, allowing dependent feelings and behavior to emerge.

In discussing differences between women and men in treatment, Dr. Brown notes that during the first year of sobriety, men appear self-confident, expressing a good deal of high self-esteem. This is consistent with a "honeymoon" period: They have high spirits immediately following the beginning of abstinence. Women, on the other hand, express their greatest feelings of low self-esteem during this period, which suggests that they do not experience the "honeymoon" phenomenon when men do. Later on, men and women appear more similar.

"One variation we've noted," says Dr. Connelly, "is that the ratio is now 66 percent male to 34 percent female, and one year we had nearly 40 percent female. We found that we had to develop special program elements for the women because their problems are different. Very often, alcoholism is precipitated or exaggerated by the empty nest syndrome. When children are reared and on their own, it's a time of crisis for many women, a time when some start drinking heavily and taking more pills to deal with the change."

Educating the alcoholic patient about aspects of her drinking is part of the program. Among the lessons taught is that alcohol is a drug, an addictive chemical that acts as a sedative for about two to four hours. Also driven home is the fact that alcohol has an agitating effect lasting from ten to twelve hours. As the sedative effect wears off, the drinker needs another to calm the increasing agitation, but with the next drink, along with the calm comes another ten to twelve hours of agitation.

Along with learning about alcohol, the patients also learn a little about themselves. Feedback from the twelve-member staff—psychologists, psychiatrists, counselors, social workers, activity therapists, and chaplains—and from fellow patients is essential to this phase. Two methods the program employs to get this feedback are role playing and self-appraisal.

The Menninger staff explains the process this way: Role playing is an attempt to get at feelings and emotions through artificially setting up potentially stressful situations. If, for example, an alcoholic patient is fearful of returning to work, role playing may involve creating a scene in which she is confronted at work by a sarcastic co-worker who taunts her about the problem drinking. Or, the drinker may play out her ambivalence and fear of returning to work or family. The patient thus has an opportunity to try different approaches to responding to these situations, and this gives her the confidence to handle future difficulties.

The staff calls self-appraisal the "hot seat," and it can be painful but illuminating. Toward the end of treatment, each patient is given a sheet of paper and asked to leave the room. She is to list what she believes to be her assets, improvements, liabilities, and any questions she might have. Meantime, the group makes out a similar list of what they believe are the individual's assets, improvements, and liabilities. When the patient returns to the room, the lists are compared. One former patient put it this way: "It's all well and good to give flowery compliments, but if we face our liabilities we see things we may not have seen before. It's hard to argue with a group of fellow patients and staff who have lived with you for four to six weeks. It can be tough. I've seen some patients break down and cry but they always come away with a much more realistic picture of themselves."

As the patients progress through the program, they gain insights into their dependency and begin to change their behavior and thinking. Because their problem drinking affects those close to them as well, family involvement is important in the treatment, and as many members as possible are encouraged to participate.

This emphasis on family participation is shared by many of the alcoholism treatment programs. Since problem drinking often does develop in a family setting, effective treatment must involve those who are part of the family, especially the spouse. "Typically," says the AMA, "the spouse appears to be the victim and also the one who tells the 'truth' about the excessive drinking. Careful scrutiny, however, may reveal this is not the whole story. The spouse may be gaining a considerable and largely unconscious payoff and will insidiously sabotage the drinker's attempts to maintain sobriety. The spouse may be in the process of recapitulating some 'ancient history' from childhood and need kind guidance to become aware of this. On the other hand, the spouse has been through so many promises only to be disappointed again that she or he is cynical and doubting.

This rebuff may give an adequate justification to the drinker to drink heavily, thus confirming the expectations of the spouse."

One daughter of an alcoholic mother, referring to her father's attitude, told us: "There have been times, after we've sobered up Mother, it would be Dad who'd give her her first drink back again. When she was on the wagon one time for three months and got upset at something he was doing, Dad said, "Oh, why don't you have a drink and calm down?" And bang, it would go on all over again. He might have had an ulterior motive. The more she drank and was out of control, the better excuse he had for screwing around, which was what he liked to do, and the more he screwed around, the more she drank."

Emily Bergson of the Appleton Treatment Center at McLean Hospital (Belmont, Massachusetts) tells us that the vast majority of patients who come to therapy are ambivalent about stopping their drinking. Pressure must be put on to help provide motivation, for if there is no significant person in the life of the alcoholic saying, "Stop" it is quite difficult for them.

"We are most fortunate when the family calls, worrying about [the] mother, for instance. She may be becoming more forgetful, or having blackouts, and the family's concern brings it to our attention. An appointment is made for the family with a member of our staff and they are encouraged to discuss the situation with the mother and invite her to come along. They tell her it would be great if she would, but if she doesn't want to they'll come anyway because they want some advice about the problem.

"We work with the alcoholic's family around creating a 'false crisis' in order to propel them into therapy while we teach a family how to intervene to maximize their leverage with the alcoholic. This can be very difficult for the family, especially when it is a woman alcoholic. Women seem to experience the stigma more—their self-esteem may suffer even more because the 'mythical alcoholic' is so at odds with most women's image of the kind of woman they want to be."[5]

The story of former First Lady Betty Ford contains all those ingredients: the initial denial, intervention by family and friends, admitting the problem, and family participation in the treatment. For fourteen years, Mrs. Ford had been taking pain medication for her arthritis and muscle spasms and had become dependent on the drugs. She also drank. "Fourteen years of being advised to take pills rather than wait for the pain to hit," she recalls. "I had never been without my drugs. I took pills for pain, I took pills to sleep, I took mild tranquilizers. Today, things are changing, doctors are educated along with the rest of us, but some of them used to be all too eager to write prescriptions. It was easier to give a woman tranquilizers and get rid of her than to sit and listen to her."

At the end of March, 1978, while her husband was on a speaking tour, Mrs. Ford was in the sitting room of the new family home in Palm Springs. Her daughter, her daughter-in-law, a family doctor, and her personal secretary all came marching in and started talking about her giving up all medication and liquor. "It was very brave of them, but I wasn't in the mood to admire them for their courage," she says. "I was completely turned off. I got very mad and was so upset that after everyone left I called a friend and complained about the terrible invasion of my privacy. I don't remember making the telephone call; the friend has told me about it."

Shortly afterward the family made a second intervention. This time her husband was there, along with her sons, a nurse, and Capt. Joseph Pursch, head of the Alcohol and Drug Rehabilitation Service at the California Naval Hospital in Long Beach. "They meant business," she recalls. "I can't remember the words. I was in shock. I've been told that Susan harked back to the days before I'd stopped drinking the first time and said she'd had to turn to Clara (who tended the Ford children) when I wasn't available; and Mike and Gayle spoke of wanting children, and wanting those children's grandmother to be healthy and in charge of her own life; and Jerry mentioned times when I'd fallen asleep in the chair at night, and times when my speech had slurred; and Steve brought up a recent weekend when he and a girlfriend had cooked dinner for me and I wouldn't come to the table on time. 'You just sat in front of the TV,' Steve said, 'and you had one drink, two drinks, three drinks. You hurt me.'

"Well, he hurt me back. All of them hurt me. I collapsed into tears. But I still had enough sense to realize they hadn't come around just to make me cry. They were there because they loved me and wanted to help me."

Despite the pressure, however, Mrs. Ford continued to resist suggestions that liquor had contributed to her illness. All she would confess to was over-medication. Capt. Pursch finally gave her a copy of the book, *Alcoholics Anonymous,* written by the founders of AA, and told her to substitute the words "chemically dependent" for "alcoholic." Shortly afterward, just two days after she turned 60, Mrs. Ford entered the Long Beach center and released a public statement saying she was determined to free herself from the damage done by pain-killers and tranquilizers. Her doctors, however, wanted her to admit she was an alcoholic. Still she resisted.

"I don't want to embarrass my husband," she said.

"You're trying to hide behind your husband," said Capt. Pursch. "Why don't you ask him if it would embarrass him if you say you're an alcoholic?"

Betty Ford remembers that she started to cry. Her husband took her hand. "There will be no embarrassment to me," he said. "You go ahead and say what should be said."

That night, while her husband lounged in a chair and read a newspaper, Mrs. Ford wrote another public statement. It said,

"I am not only addicted to the medication I have been taking for my arthritis, but also to alcohol."

Her stand prompted Capt. Pursch to remark, "Mrs. Ford is a gutsy lady, and I expect her to do very well."

While she was at Long Beach, her husband and daughter went through a two-week participatory course. They had therapy in other groups, and Betty's son, Steve, also spent a few days in the program.[6]

The Long Beach facility opened in 1970 and has cared for thousands of patients, primarily naval personnel, but including war heroes, physicians, and individuals with top-secret security clearances. The facility has also had its share of prominent patients, among them President Carter's brother, Billy, and Senator Herman Talmadge. There is no ranking of the patients, no favoritism. Admirals and seamen, the wives of former presidents and the wives of Navy pilots, all go through the same program, which is centered on small therapy groups, and each is assigned chores, such as scrubbing toilets and answering phones.

Therapy is intensive. Three hours a day of group, daily group lectures, jogging at least a mile a day, role playing, psychodrama, and nightly attendance at AA meetings in town. Meals are eaten in a public cafeteria. Treatment can stretch from six weeks to three months, and no one can check out against medical advice. Weekend passes are given out only after three weeks. Pain-killers and sleeping pills are rarely prescribed.

Treatment at the center is, of course, based on total abstinence. "Our two goals are that the patient will be totally abstinent and will return almost invariably to the same job he or she held before they came into treatment," says Capt. Pursch. "What has to be addressed is the disease of alcoholism, and the patient, no matter how important, has to be brought back to the fact that his or her basic humanness has to be addressed."[7]

The program relies heavily on AA philosophy because Pursch feels it is the best approach available. He feels that alcoholics should be exposed to AA in just the way that patients with pneumonia should be exposed to antibiotics.

The success rate at Long Beach is around 75 percent—Pursch starts to count a case as a success after two years of sobriety. The range is from 45 percent among 18- to 24-year-old-patients, to 85 to 90 percent among middle-class, middle-aged patients with families. The younger patients, it is pointed out, have a lower rate of success because they have not yet resolved their identity crises and have not yet fixed themselves professionally. The older patients are generally successful professionals.

While the Long Beach facility involves members of the alcoholic's family in the way Betty Ford's family was involved, other facilities give them an even larger role. One such facility is the Palm Beach Institute, founded in 1970 by Dr. Ronald J. Catanzaro, a psychiatrist and specialist in chemical dependencies. The Institute provides private inpatient and aftercare therapy for alcohol, drug, and other emotional problems, but by design the treatment takes place in a unique family setting where patients learn to recognize and accept the reality of their personal and family difficulties.

Catanzaro, who calls his approach "familization therapy," contends that because emotional and chemical problems are family problems, it is essential that a key member of the patient's family—spouse, parent, son, or daugher—or even a close friend—become a part of the treatment and recovery process. These close family members are designated "co-patients" and enter into therapy as residents during the latter part of the primary patient's treatment experience. (In the event that a primary patient doesn't have a key family member available as co-patient, the therapeutic team assists in developing a support system of significant others.)

"In the early phase of the program," says Catanzaro, "the

spouse would very often say, 'I don't have a drinking problem, so what do you want me here for?' It was difficult for us to simply answer, 'We suspect you're going to make so much trouble for us that we'd rather have you where we can observe you and control you rather than outside where you continue to make trouble and spoil the treatment process. In the early days, the wife would come by to bring some fresh laundry, to get the husband to sign a check, to help her pay some bills, or maybe just to complain to him that since he was sober she would like him to return home because she was lonely and it was hard to take care of the children and the house without him. The family members were constantly ripping the primary patient out of treatment and rapidly the staff was growing a full crop of gray hair from their frustrations.

"So, we finally settled on a simple rational statement to bring the spouse into therapy. We simply told her or him that as the patient got well they needed to adjust to the new way the patient was living and support her or his new life-style. But again, our thinking, as well as the family's thinking, was essentially that the real patient was the alcoholic and that the rest of us should be categorized as 'and alsos.' We were simply carried along as baggage to support the patient in her or his new way of life.

"As our experience broadened over the following years, we began changing the central theme of our concept. Our program shifted from primarily an alcoholic-oriented program to one that had a heavy emphasis on personal growth and family growth. We started admitting not only the spouse of the alcoholic, but also older children who seemed to be candidates for chemical dependency in the future or who presently were in trouble emotionally. We would admit parents of alcoholics and even employers and long-standing boyfriends or girlfriends.

"In recent years, we have shifted our emphasis to considering alcoholism as a personal illness and have gained a full appreciation that alcoholism is truly a family illness. Thus, now we consider the patient to be the whole family, whereas in former years we considered the patient to be simply the person who drank too much.

"Using this concept, we have helped families whose personal lives and whose interpersonal relationships were badly strained to form a whole new basis for living. Not only have they been encouraged to reassess their life-style and change . . . to a constructive way of living, but also we have helped them realize that the whole family as a unit needed to change its life-style. Thus, characteristically after treatment, families are far closer and can communicate on a clearer level than they have been able to do for years. Every member of the family has a greater tendency to take responsibility for the welfare of the family as well as one's own personal welfare.

"In previous years, before familization therapy concepts were fully developed, the scapegoat was always the alcoholic. If the alcoholic remained sober and lived in a way the family liked him or her to live, then the family did well. If he or she drank or was sober but did not conform to the family wishes, then it was still his or her fault that the family was doing poorly.

"With familization concepts, the family is helped to realize that everyone in the family bears a full individual responsibility for his or her own and the family's welfare, and if anything is not going right in the family, everyone must take full responsibility for the problems and for failure to correct it."[8]

The Institute, like the Long Beach facility, has had its share of prominent, wealthy patients, a fact which Daryl Kosloske, executive director, acknowledges.

"There's no question about it, we do specialize in treating a minority group," he says. "Most people in our culture don't view the affluent as a minority group, [but] they are, just like Chicanos, just like Blacks. I think the families themselves end up keeping the alcoholic sicker longer because they're in the limelight. They have to keep an image up. They're tough to get into treatment. And some of them are tough to treat because they have kind of an overwhelming ego—the Big I syndrome."[9] Among its patients have been Wilbur Mills, who spent some time there after his well-publicized fling with Fanne Fox, and Ruby Folsom Austin, mother of Cornelia Wallace. Mrs. Wallace told us about her mother's treatment:

I've learned . . . that there are five roles in alcoholism that are played by various members of the family. One is the alcoholic, two is the victim, three is the persecutor, four is the scapegoat, and five is the rescuer. I knew I played the rescuer, but also I know I played the persecutor. I persecuted Mother. I'd say, "Well, you know, if you hadn't been drinkin' when such and such was goin' on. . . ." I'd get aggravated, and I'd say things like, "You've been drinkin' so hard how do you expect to do this, or remember that?" That's persecution, beatin' her over the head about her past drinkin' and I don't want to do that, it's not healthy.

But, you see, if I hadn't gone through this program, I'd do it and not know that I had. Now, I may still do it (and it does slip out occasionally), but I know what I've done and I say, "I shouldn't. . . ."

Two, six, twelve weeks of treatment aren't going to change those very subtle things. You have to get better progressively, by being aware and checkin' yourself. The awareness is what you get in the program. This is the way it is. Take a look at what you're doin', what part you're playin'. "How am I goin' to keep from doin' that?" I'd say, because that's so subtle . . . Changin' those roles, those habits, those ways of relating is just hard as the devil. . . .

It's almost harder to change those patterns of behavior as it is for her to stop drinkin'. I don't know, but it's probably easier just to give up the alcohol than to change the pattern or behavior, the way of relating. It's really just learnin' a new way of communicating, of showin' love, of caring about you and comin' at you straight on instead of manipulating. . . .

Mother and I really had a lot of fun together. We've done some fun things, and I like her. She's delightful but much more so and nicer to be around without alcohol. She created a lot of financial problems for us there, get behind in her house payments, and I'd have to go over there and pay them off and so on, and that's the rescuer. And you'd hear [people] say, "Well, just let 'em hit rock bottom and they'll bottom out." But you know, I don't want my mother to hit rock bottom. I love my mother and I want to save her from herself because she can't save herself . . . and she couldn't because she was addicted, couldn't quit if she wanted. That's what her husband said, and he was a doctor. They were up there at a Virginia place with a team of psychiatrists comin' in every month and I'd kept tellin' 'em, she needs treatment. . . .[10]

Many programs, we have said, either use or are based on the Alcoholics Anonymous approach to achieving and maintaining sobriety. AA is undoubtedly the best known and probably the most effective therapy, a fellowship (one can call it a sisterhood considering the fact that some chapters have more women than men) in which members meet in a group therapy setting of honesty and camaraderie. The participants freely admit their drinking problems and describe their personal experiences, acknowledging that alcoholism is not a happy state, but yet not a disgrace. The only requirement for membership is a desire to quit drinking. There are no dues or fees, and AA is not allied with any religious denomination or institution.

AA has chosen to identify alcoholism as a disease or an addiction to a powerful sedative drug, resembling the situation of a diabetic who craves sugar. At the same time, the organization agrees that any of the other theories about its cause may be true in whole or in part.

A key element in AA is the twenty-four-hour program, which simply boils down to this: "We ask the Power that we recognize as being greater than ourselves (in most cases God as we understand God) in the morning to help us go through twenty-four hours without a drink. And at the end of the day, we thank that Power for helping us. The next day the same procedure is followed. It is repeated each succeeding day until we find that these twenty-four hour periods have grown to weeks and months, our thinking is clearer, and we are better able to consider practicing more of the twelve steps [rules of conduct which the organization believes to be the way to recovery] in our daily lives. It might be difficult in your present state of mind to realize that your thinking has anything to do with your drinking. But we have found this to be so."

AA believes that, when the program is energetically and honestly followed, failure is not possible—provided the person is not mentally impaired and is truly determined to give up drinking. The organization further feels that its case histories prove the validity of its claim.

However, the 45-year-old organization is not without its critics, despite the popularity of its approach. Recently, sociologist Robert Tournier charged that AA has "come to dominate alcoholism both as an ideology and as a method" and AA's assumptions about the nature of alcohol dependence "have virtually been accepted as fact by most of those in the field." He writes that AA's influence over the treatment field "has fettered innovation, precluded early intervention, and tied us to a treatment strategy which, in addition to reaching only a small portion of problem drinkers, is limited in its applicability to the universe of alcoholics."[11]

There was also this anonymous comment in a 1979 issue of *The Journal,* the monthly publication of the Addiction Research Foundation of Toronto:

"Although AA is justifiably praised for its pioneering role in the treatment of alcohol-related problems, it has evolved over the course of time into a reactionary organization which, at present, exercises a stultifying effect upon the field. In particular, its claim of universal therapeutic efficacy is patently false and its hysterical acts upon alternative treatment philosophies wholly unwarranted. They give undue credence to the disease concept of alcoholism, but this is perhaps inevitable given the difficulties involved in maintaining abstinence. . . .

"AA has failed to retain many alcoholics as members partly because of its religious bias, but mainly because of its insistence that alcoholics are fundamentally different from you and me. . . . It is one of the few movements that capitalizes on the powers of social pressure and social organization, which are the real controllers of people's behavior. It raises the question as to whether the one-on-one approach of typical medical and psychological intervention could ever be effective."

This question also arises: Is AA effective for women?

Some women maintain that the organization does little to help because of its male orientation; that women need more than that because of their special difficulties with alcohol; that AA is more effective for "traditional" women than for today's liberated women. Lesbians, too, generally feel that AA does not meet their alcohol-dependent needs because the issue of their homosexuality is difficult to face for most AA members.

One woman who does not believe that AA helps women very much is Dr. Jean Kirkpatrick, founder of Women for Sobriety, Inc., a program designed to help women alcoholics develop a sense of self-esteem and positive attitudes in everyday life. When she decided to quit drinking, she joined AA—twice. Both times it failed.

"Women alcoholics need something additional to AA," she says. "Their problems go deeper than men's. They feel they've failed as wives, as mothers, as daughters, and as women. They carry great burdens of guilt from the feeling of failure. . . . AA takes a spiritual look at overcoming alcohol. Women for Sobriety emphasizes that we are totally responsible for our own self-image."

The female-oriented group is organized like AA and is run by its own local chapter members. The members are encouraged to also join AA as well as any other anti-alcoholic groups that they can for support. "When you're an alcoholic, you need all the help you can get," says Kirkpatrick. "There's only one end to alcohol—that's death, whether you are a man or a woman."

Kirkpatrick says that despite AA's great successes, only 6 to 10 percent of all alcoholics ever join, and only 3.5 to 5 percent of all women alcoholics ever do.

"The Women for Sobriety Program is an affirmation of the value and worth of each woman," she says. "It is a program that leads each woman to asserting her belief in self, a program that leads her to seeing herself in a positive and self-confident image. She will see herself as forceful and compassionate, assertive and warm, capable and caring, resourceful and responsible. The Women for Sobriety program centers on the woman as the AA program cannot do, because it was not intended to. Historically, the AA program came into being when it was still believed that very few women had a drinking problem. Today we know that there are as many women alcoholics as men, and as women assume more responsible positions in this fast-paced society, their number is growing."[12]

AA has, as noted, its twelve steps upon which members model their lives. WFS has thirteen statements of acceptance. We present both:

Alcoholics Anonymous

We:

1. Admitted we were powerless over alcohol, that our lives had become unmanageable.

2. Came to believe that a power greater than ourselves could restore us to sanity.

3. Made a decision to turn our will and our lives over to the care of God as we understand Him.

4. Made a searching and fearless moral inventory of ourselves.

5. Admitted to God, to ourselves, and to another human being the exact nature of our wrongs.

6. Were entirely ready to have God remove all these defects of character.

7. Humbly asked Him to remove our shortcomings.

8. Made a list of all persons we had harmed, and became willing to make amends to them all.

9. Made direct amends to such people wherever possible, except when to do so would injure them or others.

10. Continued to take personal inventory, and when we were wrong promptly admitted it.

11. Sought through prayer and meditation to improve our conscious contact with God as we understand Him, praying only for knowledge of His will and the power to carry that out.

12. Having had a spiritual experience as the result of these steps, we tried to carry this message to alcoholics, and to practice these principles in all our affairs.

Women for Sobriety

1. I have a drinking problem that once had me.

2. Negative emotions destroy only myself.

3. Happiness is a habit I will develop.

4. Problems bother me only to the degree I permit them to.

5. I am what I think.

6. Life can be ordinary or it can be great.

7. Love can change the course of my world.

8. The fundamental object of life is emotional and spiritual growth.

9. The past is gone forever.

10. All love given returns two-fold.

11. Enthusiasm is my daily exercise.

12. I am a competent woman and have much to give others.

13. I am responsible for myself and my sisters.

"The thirteen statements," says Kirkpatrick, "provide a way of viewing life . . . that differs from earlier defensive behavioral response. It is a form of reality therapy that changes the alcoholic woman's negative defensiveness to positive action through a learning of self."

WHERE TO FIND HELP

Listed below are the names, addresses, and telephone numbers of the major organizations, both public and private, that deal with problem drinking. They offer information about alcohol use and abuse and will also, in many cases, provide information on state and local resources. However, for more complete information on your local alcoholism treatment centers, check with your state's Department of Public Health or Mental Health, as well as your community mental health center and/or women's health centers. Also check your telephone yellow pages directory under "Alcoholism Information and Treatment Centers."

Al-Anon Family Group Headquarters, Inc.
P.O. Box 182
Madison Square Station
New York, NY 10010   Tel.: 212-481-6565

Alcoholics Anonymous World Services, Inc.
P.O. Box 459
Grand Central Station
New York, NY 10017   Tel.: 212-686-1100

National Center for Alcohol Education
1601 North Kent Street
Arlington, VA 22209   Tel.: 703-527-5757

National Council on Alcoholism, Inc.
733 Third Avenue
New York, NY 10017   Tel.: 212-986-4433

National Institute on Alcohol Abuse and Alcoholism
National Clearinghouse for Alcohol Information
P.O. Box 2345
Rockville, MD 20852   Tel.: 301-468-2600

Women for Sobriety, Inc.
P.O. Box 618
Quakertown, PA 18951   Tel.: 215-536-8026

The following is an updated list of women's alcoholism treatment programs funded by the National Institute on Alcohol Abuse and Alcoholism:

Women's Rehabilitation Association
   of San Mateo County, Inc.
122 Second Ave., Suite 210
San Mateo, CA 94401   Tel.: 415-343-5019 or
Leona M. Kent   415-348-6603

Casa de Las Amigas
160 N. El Molina Avenue
Pasadena, CA 91106
Marilyn A. Sachs   Tel.: 213-792-2770

Council on Alcoholism
206 Wm. Howard Taft Road
Cincinnati, OH 45219
Carol A. Wambaugh   Tel.: 513-281-7882

Addiction Treatment Division
Centre House, 16th Floor
1400 N.W. 10th Avenue
Miami, FL 33136
James A. Ward   Tel.: 305-324-7100

Cape Cod Alcoholism Intervention and
   Rehabilitation Unit, Inc.
P.O. Drawer P, 870 County Road
Pocasset, MA 02559
Paul Rothfeld   Tel.: 617-563-7101

Columbia Point Alcoholism Program, Inc.
100 Monticello Avenue
Dorchester, MA 02125
William R. Loesch   Tel.: 617-282-0871

Alcoholism Services of Greater Springfield, Inc.
c/o Opportunity House, Inc.
P.O. Box 1444
Springfield, MA 01104
Nancy B. Fisk   Tel.: 413-739-4732

Alcoholism Center for Women, Inc.
1147 South Alvarado Street
Los Angeles, CA 90006
Travis H. Foote   Tel.: 213-381-7805

Pine Tree Alcoholism Treatment Center for Women, Inc.
1040 Main Street
South Windham, ME 04082
John T. Nugent   Tel.: 207-892-2192

The Women's Alcoholism Program of CASPAR, Inc.
1348 Cambridge Street
Cambridge, MA 02139
Norma Finkelstein   Tel.: 617-661-1316

San Juan Health Department
San Juan Municipal Hospital
Box B.R.
Puerto Rico Medical Center
Rio Piedras, PR 00925
Ivonne A. Cordero-Muratti   Tel.: 809-766-5172

St. Monica's Home
6420 Colby Street
Lincoln, NB 68505
Patricia R. Wall   Tel.: 402-466-9067

Butler County Commissioner's Council on Drug
  and Alcohol Abuse
300 S. Washington Street
Butler, PA 16001
David C. Campbell   Tel.: 412-287-8205

Eagleville Hospital and Rehabilitation Center
P.O. Box 45
Eagleville, PA 19408
Donald J. Ottenberg, M.D.   Tel.: 215-539-6000

The Harbinger, Inc.
1401 N.E. 70th Street
Oklahoma City, OK 73111
Margo E. Halford   Tel.: 405-478-2809

Chrysalis, A Center for Women
2104 Stevens Avenue, South
Minneapolis, MN 55404
Karen A. Sartin   Tel.: 612-871-0118

Howard County Health Department
3450 Court House Drive
Ellicott City, MD 21043
Florence Rowley   Tel.: 301-465-5000

7

Drinking
RESPONSIBLY

Sometimes I just want a drink and I feel like I'm going crazy if I don't have one . . . Those are the times I try to make sure I don't have one.

Eleanor, 42, mother of two and wife of a
tavern owner

There are some individuals who will tell you, in all sincerity, that if you want to avoid a drinking problem, just don't drink. Easier said than done. Such advice is like saying that the best form of birth control is a one-word answer when you feel the urge to have sex: "No."

Alcohol alone does not cause alcoholism, no more than watching movie violence causes us to commit a crime, or smoking marijuana automatically transforms us into dope addicts. Although it's obvious that there would be no problem drinking without alcohol, laying the blame on it alone is the same as blaming marriage for divorce.

Millions of drinkers enjoy all manner of alcoholic beverages, and the vast majority do so without any adverse effect whatsoever, and are not dependent on them. What is important is the pattern and purpose of drinking, how and why we drink. There is wide agreement on this point, and we cannot emphasize enough that if you really understand the difference between responsible and irresponsible drinking patterns, if you are aware of the warning signs that can tell you to be cautious, and if you know the essential facts about how alcohol works in your body, then you don't have to become an alcoholic or a problem drinker. One drink, if you've never had one before, will not force you to down the whole bottle through some bizarre reaction of biochemistry, or cause you to be forever hooked. Nor do regular cocktails in a relaxed setting—that drink or two before dinner each night that can lighten the day's tensions and settle you down—mean that you're on the road to becoming alcoholic. Addiction is infinitely more complex than that, as we have seen.

Alcohol is, and has been known as such for a long, long time, an effective social lubricant and tranquilizer that, when used sensibly, can enhance our enjoyment of life. It is, says Dr. Morris Chafetz, the only substance in medicine that has both a drug action and food value, and that can provide energy and sedation simultaneously. "The energy that alcohol provides is at a minimal cost to the body, since it does not require digestion," he says.[1] Wine, especially, with its many vitamins and minerals in addition to its mild alcoholic content, has singular beneficial properties that make it, in the view of many physicians, an excellent supplementary source, as well as a safe, natural calmative.

Cognac, which is brandy distilled from wine or fermented fruit juice, provides energy through its carbohydrate content and its simple sugars, which are stored as glycogen and converted into glucose when the body requires more energy. Other nutritional constituents of cognac include calcium, iron, and sodium, all derived from the original soil in which cognac grapes grow, along with pectins, purines, fats, dextrose, and levalose.

Wine (and beer) are served in many hospitals and nursing homes in the United States. In fact, psychologists studied the interpersonal behavior of elderly patients who had been allowed to partake moderately and found that they became more socially involved with one another, formed friendships more easily and, in general, enjoyed a greater sense of togetherness and security. Even those who study alcoholism and the ill effects of alcohol admit that wine can be used advantageously in geriatrics. A Yale group has observed:

"There is one condition, however, in which the utility of alcoholic beverages, in suitable moderation and low concentrations, is generally admitted, and that is the bodily discomforts brought about by old age. The desire for food is increased; there is a mild euphoria, a cheerfulness, and a decrease of anxiety; the feeling of chilliness is lessened by the flow of blood to the skin; and the mild sedative action of the alcohol relieves some of the aches and pains. Very small amounts of alcoholic beverages may add greatly to the comfort and peace of mind of the aged."

Wine has also been used to control high blood pressure in patients, and there is some evidence that red wines in particular are capable of lowering dangerous cholesterol levels through the action of complex substances called polyphenols, which they contain in abundance. Wine also sometimes helps regulate the heartbeat, is an effective appetite stimulant, is a diuretic, has antibiotic properties, and may be used to treat malabsorption syndrome, a disorder in which the ability to absorb fat from the digestive tract is decreased.

Distilled spirits, too, may have value in moderate amounts, not only as a psychological relaxer, but through their direct effect as vasodilators—enlargers of blood vessels—which can relieve or prevent angina pectoris, the pain in the chest that is caused by a spasm of the heart's coronary artery. The 18th-century physician William Heberden was the first to recognize and advocate the use of alcohol for the relief of angina, advice which the late Dr. Paul Dudley White, of Harvard Medical School and the Massachusetts General Hospital, also gave. Only an ounce or two of distilled liquor, White wrote, may bring rapid relief from angina pain, often in a very few minutes.

Recent research has also suggested that moderate amounts of alcohol increase levels of a "good" form of cholesterol (HDL, a high-density fat that many clinicians believe protects against heart disease) and reduce the amount of "bad" cholesterol—low-density lipoprotein. In fact, several studies have shown that moderate drinkers die less often from cardiovascular problems than do either teetotalers or heavy drinkers. Moderate drinkers, also, seem to live longer in general than both heavy drinkers and those who don't drink at all.

Of course, none of what we have said should be taken to mean that drinking is fine for everyone. Some people simply don't wish to drink; they don't like the taste or they're physically allergic to alcohol. It's also important to remember that alcohol is never to be considered a treatment for any disorder, physical or psychological. It does not cure heart disease or cancer, nor can it relieve your depression. Apart from the fact that there is always some laboratory evidence that presents an opposing view—a recent study at the Cleveland Clinic, for example, found no difference in the HDL levels of abstainers and moderate drinkers, only of those who drank more than four drinks a day—we must emphasize that the addicted individual, or one who shows signs of becoming dependent, must be wary. "There is no doubt that the dangers of acute or chronic excessive alcohol intake far outweigh any theoretical beneficial effect of HDL cholesterol," said a recent advisory by the American Heart Association Nutrition Committee. "The best way to reduce your level of blood cholesterol is to eat a prudent diet that is low in fat and eggs, which are the main sources of cholesterol."

Along these lines, Dr. W. P. Castelli of the National Heart Institute in Framingham, Massachusetts said recently that it may be dangerous to tell some people to take two drinks a day when, given their constitutional makeup, one could fairly predict they could not stop at two. "Thus, what started out as prudent advice turned into advice that led to cardiac death by alcoholic cardiomyopathy rather than to an extension of life by lowering coronary atherosclerosis," he pointed out in a November, 1979, editorial in the *Journal of the American Medical Association.* "With seventeen million alcoholics in this country, we perhaps have a message for which this country is not yet ready," he concludes.

Alcohol should not be drunk by individuals suffering from stomach disorders such as gastritis, ulcers, or gastric cancer, nor by those with liver disease, kidney infections, pancreatitis, epilepsy, throat irritations, and a number of other conditions that a physician, after careful evaluation, feels would prohibit its use. There are also, as already mentioned, the reactions that can be produced when alcohol is mixed with various medications.

However, alcohol has its place, and that, essentially, is the message we hope we have conveyed. But its place—the role it plays in making our lives more pleasurable—is shaky if it is not grounded in an awareness of the risks involved, a recognition of the warning signals that alert us to those risks, and a healthy regard for moderation in drinking behavior.

Margo works on an assembly line in an electronics factory in San Jose. Her father, she says, never touched a drop in his life, although his father was an alcoholic. Her mother buys a pint of cordial once a year and sips it on holidays only. Margo is 29, never drank in high school, and now considers herself a "sensible drinker":

I tend to drink only when I'm in a social environment. When I go home at night from the plant, I don't drink at all then, never. I drink only on weekends, when people come over, and I could go for three, four weekends in a row without a visitor and we'd not have one drink at all. But as soon as someone comes by for the weekend—and we usually have a lot of people over—it's, "Hey, what are you drinking?"

Every one of my women friends is like that. We're all hitting 30, and most don't have any children, and we're all in situations where we feel we work hard during the week and we want to hang looser on weekends. And the way to do it, we feel, is to have friends in and drink together.

With the guys, it's a little different. The husbands . . . get out of work, and every night they stop off for a few on the way home. Sometimes, [my husband] picks me up at work, and if he gets out earlier, he's had a few and that makes me mad as hell. Here I've just worked hard, maybe twelve hours for some OT, and although I don't begrudge him enjoying himself—he's put in a tough day, too—it does bother me. I don't really let him know, though, because it's the sort of thing a man does, that's all. You just accept it.

But I do, really, associate drinking with a social environment. Last night, for instance, my husband had this craving for Italian food, so while we were waiting for a table he said, "Let's go into the bar," which is something we rarely do. Well, I sat down and I had a drink, and I really didn't enjoy it very much. I really don't enjoy drinking if I'm just sitting there. The drinks on those occasions . . . seem . . . secondary. But with my friends, it's very different. I cannot imagine spending a weekend with my friends and not drinking. I mean, they become so much more fun after a few drinks. They become more witty and they do crazy things . . .

Sometimes, though, there is much too much drinking, among the women especially—to the point where some of them can't control themselves, to the point where they can't walk or talk straight. Once in a while, that happens, yes. I'm concerned about the ones who do it all the time.

Strangely enough, ten drinks, which I've done many times, leaves me usually what I consider to be sober. I'm still functioning, still talking, still hostessing. I don't know why I have this capacity, but I do. I know I can go up to four weeks without liquor, and if I were an al-

coholic I wouldn't be able to do that—I'd have to have it all the time. But then I figure, it's not a question of how much, but where and how you drink it.

I'm also a proud person, I guess. I have a fairly responsible job at the plant, supervising the line, forty-five or so people, and I have to have some dignity about myself. I have this pride, and I don't want people to see me in a bad way, out of control. And I really feel that what keeps me sober even after all that liquor is my will, my determination not to let myself go like some of the others. I do think it has a lot to do with personality, I really do.

In my group, I'm comfortable, they're all my friends. I can drink, and I mean this, all day long without getting drunk. But you know, if I'm with people that I don't dare let myself go with, or that I don't know very well, I drink one drink and I'm gone, my words slur, I'm conscious of what I'm doing, I start to trip over myself. . . . With [my friends], I'm in control. But put me with strangers, and I'm a different person.

If you drink, there is always the potential danger that alcohol might contribute to some difficulty later on. We have already made clear the risks—addiction, of course, being the principal danger. How do you know whether you are at risk? There are ways to determine whether you are on the road to addiction or problem drinking, but bear in mind that no test that relies on human behavior as an indicator can be as exact as a brain scan or a blood test.

Monitoring the levels of HDL cholesterol in the blood might be one way to do it scientifically, but there are pitfalls in that method: Some individuals have high HDL levels whether they drink or not. Also, an HDL test might merely reflect the quantity of alcohol consumed, which as we suggested earlier, is not always a good indicator of a potential alcohol problem.

Doctors are also alerted to look for certain physical clues that might signal a drinking problem. Heartburn is one; vomiting before breakfast is another, along with morning cough, increased pulse rate, high blood pressure, tremors in middle age, bruises that might have been caused by stumbling, frequent accidents, anxiety, tension, insomnia, an enlarged liver, and high blood sugar. But these, again, might appear in the nonalcoholic as well, and they are really not the sort of symptoms that would be of much help for the woman who wants to determine whether she is at risk. You can't always tell by examining a person whether she has a drinking problem, nor can you do it with an X-ray or an EKG.

The following questions might help you to at least think twice about your drinking habits; start disciplining yourself a little more; or, if need be, seek professional help. However, no one can say firmly that answering "Yes" to one or three or all of the questions is proof that you have a problem.

1. Do you often think and talk about drinking, or have a daily desire to drink?

2. Do you "bottoms-up" your drinks, tossing them down quickly, or chug-a-lug your beers? Do you always finish your glass of wine before everyone else at dinner?

3. Do you drink more heavily when you're tense, or when you need to relax?

4. Lately, have you extended your evening cocktail hour and added in an extra drink or two?

5. Have the occasional business lunch cocktails of the past become a daily pre-luncheon ritual?

6. Do you ever feel edgy or disappointed if no drinks are served at a party, or do you go out socially only if you know you're going to drink?

7. Are you in the habit of drinking by yourself?

8. Do you ever forget what you or anybody you were with did while you drank? Did someone have to get you home?

9. Do you ever hide liquor?

10. Has anybody ever told you that you drink too much, and you denied it? Has anyone ever suggested that you take it easy, and you laughed off the advice?

11. Do you drink to get drunk, regularly telling your friends, "Let's get bombed"?

12. Do you drink in the morning, either to get started or to relieve a hangover?

13. Do you become argumentative or depressed, or get into fights when you're drinking? Do you feel you're wittier or sexier?

14. Have you missed work or school or a recreational event because you've been drunk or hung-over?

15. Have you ever been arrested or had an accident because of your drinking?

16. Do you change package stores regularly to cover up the amount of liquor you buy?

17. Do you drink before the guests arrive?

18. Do you carry liquor in your purse or keep it in your desk drawer?

19. Do you plan to reward yourself with a drink after a stressful day?

20. Do you avoid discussing alcohol problems with others but read about alcoholics or alcoholism when you're alone?

21. Do you find that you will pass up meals while drinking?

22. Do you get frightened after you've drunk a lot?

23. Do you become overly nice to your family and friends in order to make up to them for things you might have said or done while drinking?

24. Do you dispose secretly of your empties?

25. Have you ever been hospitalized for a problem that, when you think about it honestly, could have been related to your drinking?

Another test you can take, once or twice a year, is to quit drinking for at least a week. No cocktails, no wine with your meals, no beer at the outdoor barbecue. If you can do it without missing it or without experiencing withdrawal symptoms—the jitters, irritability, feeling that your body actually needs liquor—then you're probably all right. If you cannot even conceive of making such a test, or if you find ways to postpone trying it, then you may be closer to trouble than you realize.

Boston City Hospital, as part of its routine prenatal clinic examination, asks female patients to fill out a simple questionnaire. Designed by Dr. Henry Rosett and his colleagues as part of their investigation into the fetal alcohol syndrome, it has been administered to more than 1500 patients and has proven extremely accurate in identifying women with drinking problems.

The questionnaire is printed on a small slip of paper that can be stapled to the clinical record. The questions ask:

• Smoking: How many packs per day?

• Beer: How many times per week?

• How many cans each time?

• Ever drink more?

• Wine: How many times per week?

• How many glasses each time?

• Ever drink more?

• Liquor: How many times per week?

• How many drinks each time?

•   Ever drink more?

Lyn Weiner, a member of Dr. Rosett's team, says they qualify a person who drinks forty-five drinks or more per month, or six drinks per occasion, as a heavy drinker. A person who almost never drinks is a rare drinker, and everybody else classifies as moderate.

It's not always easy to recognize the signs of problem drinking. Remember that alcoholism or problem drinking doesn't strike you like lightning, without warning. When you do start to show signs of drinking irresponsibly, they may be vague and won't necessarily interfere with your job or your relationships with others. Even if you are drinking more, you may not notice anything wrong or out of the ordinary and rationalize that you can stop anytime you want, or that the problem will take care of itself. You also may not recognize the signals, because alcohol can alter your judgment just enough to actually hide the changes in your drinking behavior from you.

The pattern of denying the situation or overlooking the signals is often more evident in women drinkers. Because of conditioning—the expectation that she "act like a woman"—a woman tends to cover up more in order to soften the image that drinking has given her and to bring back the ideal she is supposed to mirror. Others, who know that their wife or mother or girlfriend is beginning to answer "Yes" to many of the aforementioned questions, also ignore the answers, and thus another avenue to treatment or behavior modification is blocked.

The questions we've asked should give you some hint about how, when, and where you ought to drink. The goals are drinking responsibly and avoiding intoxication, both of which should make alcohol a pleasant adjunct to life, not a crutch to make it bearable. This message is not new. "Make not thyself helpless in drinking in the beer shop," declared the writer of the Precepts of Ani, a 3,000-year-old Egyptian book of amenities. "For will not the words of thy report repeated slip out from thy mouth without thy knowing that thou hast uttered them? Falling down, thy limbs will be broken, and no one will give thee a hand to help thee up. As for thy companions in the swilling of beer, they will get up and say, 'Outside with this drunkard.'"

Even Dr. Benjamin Rush, who spoke out against "ardent spirits" as agents that lead women and men to disease, debt, and the gallows, had no quarrel with milder alcoholic beverages in moderation and saw them as entirely compatible with health, long life, and respectability. Still another past advocate of moderation and responsible drinking was Dr. R. V. Pierce of the Invalids' Hotel and Surgical Institute of Buffalo, who in 1909 wrote an immensely popular volume, *The People's Common Sense Medical Adviser in Plain English.* Here's what the doctor had to say on the subject: "It will be said that alcohol cheers the weary and that to take a little wine for the stomach's sake is one of the lessons that comes from the deep recesses of human nature. I am not so obstinate to deny this argument. There are times in the life of man when the heart is oppressed, when the resistance to its motion is excessive, and when blood flows languidly to the centres of life, nervous and muscular. In these moments alcohol cheers. It lets loose the heart from its oppression; it lets flow a brisker current of blood into the failing organs; it aids nutritive changes, and altogether is of temporary service to man. So far, alcohol may be good, and if its use could be limited to this one action, this one purpose, it would be amongst the most excellent of the gifts of science to mankind. . . .

"The true place of alcohol is clear; it is an agreeable temporary shroud. The savage, with the mansions of his soul unfurnished, buries his restless energy under its shadow. The civilized man, overburdened with mental labor or with engrossing care, seeks the same shade; but it is shade, after all, in which, in exact proportion as he seeks it, the seeker retires from perfect natural life. To search for force in alcohol is, to my mind, equivalent to the act of seeking for the sun in subterranean gloom until it is night."

Pierce's message, 70 years old, is appropriate today, provided we add in the feminine pronoun. In a 1974 resource book initiated by the American Association for Health, Physical Education and Recreation, a national affiliate of the National Education Association, there is this further commentary on sensible drinking habits:

"For those who understand their reasons for drinking and who choose to drink, the key to drinking with low-risk potential (responsible behavior) can be summarized in one sentence. For any person, to drink with low-risk potential means to know himself and his own limitations in regard to drinking (to have a high self-esteem) and to consciously control drinking.

"In a sense, the inculcation of this attitude is opposite to that involved in most other learning situations, in which students are encouraged to think, in the words of the poet Robert Browning, that 'a man's reach should exceed his grasp.' For alcohol education, we would suggest that if a person makes a choice to drink, his reach should *not* exceed his grasp.

"Though any one person's reach may differ from that of his fellow men, there are general guidelines that apply to all people who choose to drink in a responsible manner."

Following are some things you should do when you drink in order to get the most benefit at the least risk:

• Limit and measure your drinks. Don't try to do what the men do—that is, equating drinking capacity with success. If you're new to the corporate world, for example, you're at risk not only because of the pressures of the business lunch with its traditional cocktails, but because you are a woman and the need to do as they do might make you careless. One good rule to use is Anstie's Limit, named after the British psychiatrist, Sir Francis Anstie, who defined moderate daily drinking as about three ounces of liquor (three conventional "shot" glasses of distilled spirits), or half a bottle of wine, or four eight-ounce glasses of beer, taken only with meals. But be wary of "jigger" measurements, which contain an ounce and a half of liquor, and "doubles," which can amount to two or three ounces of liquor depending on the measure used. That "one drink" that you limit yourself to might be the size of your morning glass of orange juice if you or your host or hostess are careless.

• Mix your drinks with water, fruit juice, or plenty of ice. This dilutes the alcohol and slows down its absorption into your bloodstream. When sweet fruit juices are used as mixers, they also tend to weaken the kick, because the fructose they contain burns off the alcohol faster. All other things being equal, this should forestall drunkeness.

Although women have traditionally drunk such "mixed" drinks, sometimes overemphasizing the creamy, sweetened, fruity concoctions that might cause less trouble than straight stuff, their drinking preferences have recently changed. More and more women—because they are emulating the male drinking patterns, because they realize that straight liquor is indeed quicker, or because they prefer it—have turned to martinis straight up, to bourbons and whiskeys and Scotches on the rocks, "but very light on the ice."

Be careful of soda, tonic water and every other carbonated mixer. They increase the rate of absorption because of their carbon dioxide content, and the result is that the alcohol in your drink is sped toward the brain faster. This is why Champagne and other sparkling wines can affect you quicker than the noneffervescent or "still" wines.

• Drink slowly. This is very important because it takes about an hour for that half-ounce of pure alcohol in an ounce of liquor, a can of beer, or a glass of wine to be oxidized. Thus, you might easily have one drink an hour for twenty-four hours (a theoretical situation that no one advises because of the damage that consistent heavy drinking can do) and still remain reasonably sober. If you're out for a "few beers" with the guys, define "a few" as two, and sip.

• Always be aware of your physiology. Chances are you will become intoxicated more quickly and on less alcohol than a man. Be wary of drinking too much after your menstrual period because, as we said earlier, the lower level of hormones makes you get drunk quicker. The same advice holds true if you are menopausal.

•   If you're taking medication, know what it's doing in your body. If you're on estrogen for contraception or to replace the hormone lost during menopause, be careful because you'll be metabolizing alcohol more slowly.

•   Eat before or while you drink. This slows the rate at which alcohol is absorbed into the bloodstream, gentling its effects, and it also slows up a non-stop drinker. The usual "munchies" aren't the best food barriers, however. If you're hostessing, serve snacks high in protein: cheese, seafoods, meats, deviled eggs.

If you're going to be out drinking, it's not a bad idea to put something of the sort, or a glass of milk, into your stomach beforehand. Protein foods retard absorption because, for one thing, they remain in the stomach a lot longer than other foods. Another trick is to eat canapé crackers or toast spread with honey while you drink or afterward. This will speed up oxidation of the alcohol in your system.

•   Stick with the "safer" drinks when circumstances are working against you—for example, when your estrogen-progesterone levels are lower or when you're tired and hungry. Although you can boost the effect of any alcoholic beverage simply by drinking more of it, remember that there is less alcohol per bottle in wine and beer than in hard liquors. Dinner wines, such as Chablis, Burgundy, and Zinfandel, and Chianti, sherry and port contain considerably less alcohol than distilled liquors.

Sipping a small—and the emphasis is on small—glass of vermouth or Chablis is safer than sipping a martini, all other factors being equal. We also tend to take wine with meals, which makes it less potent. Beer, quite fashionable among young women these days, is also classified as a "safer" drink because it contains even less alcohol than wine, is usually consumed more slowly than liquor, and has a number of ingredients that slow its action in the body.

• Consider your frame of mind when you drink, because this can play a part in how fast alcohol affects you. As Dr. Morris Chafetz has said in his book, *Why Drinking Can Be Good For You,* alcohol does the most for you when you choose the time, place, and circumstances of drinking rather carefully: "Now, obviously, if you are going to be writing, driving, filling out a tax form, or engaged in any other highly complex mental or physical activity, it scarcely seems appropriate to be under the influence of an anesthetic drug. On the other hand, if you're going to be sharing a meal or enjoying human interchange, just sitting around in a relaxed way, then alcohol can be a terrific adjunct to the essential human experience of socializing. It's then that alcohol is at its best, a true servant of man.

"The Chinese sip their alcohol, savoring each drop as a gift of God, and they drink to celebrate their mutual interdependence. Drunkenness and alcoholism are almost unknown in China. Having observed safe and healthy drinking practices in many parts of the world, I've learned that where alcohol is used in the Chinese style, people generally reap its great gifts while avoiding its pain."

• Try to avoid standing when you drink. Sit down comfortably and drink with a friend, and you'll find that the alcohol won't affect you as drastically as it would at a frantic cocktail party, where you drink a lot faster and therefore a lot more, where encountering one person after another might make you anxious.

• If you're the hostess, try to be aware of the drinking habits of your guests. You're not really doing anyone a favor by overloading the punch or keeping an open bar. See that snacks are passed around often, that soft drinks are available for those who can't or don't wish to drink alcohol, and stick to the limits of your cocktail hour by announcing dinner promptly. If no meal is to be served, state the time for cocktails on your invitation and stand by it. If that doesn't work and the party shows signs of continuing far beyond your expectations, you can always conveniently run out of liquor. Tell a close friend to help you start passing the word, or make your own later plans for the evening known to your guests.

Concern for yourself is not the only reason you should impose a limit. As a hostess you're responsible for seeing that your guests get home safely, so it's to your advantage to avoid rushing refills and to pay attention to how people are behaving.

While many women may not necessarily appreciate the philosophy of an all-male organization, the U.S. Jaycees, through its Operation Threshold, a collaborative endeavor with the NIAAA, views responsible drinking in an admirable way:

"Responsible drinking can be honorable, safe, healthy, and sensible, and reflects alcohol's use for the enjoyment of life rather than a crutch against it. It involves intention and attitude more than just correct mechanical things. In a deeper sense it may reveal your personal outlook on life. And your outlook on life takes into account your upbringing, value system, life-style, religious feelings, age, maturity, experiences, living skills, and responsibility. In the final analysis, anyone choosing to drink has a responsibility not to destroy himself or society.

"Parents or teachers who do not allow realistic and scientifically sound discussion about responsible drinking; hospital administrators, clergymen, and legislators who do not believe alcoholism is a treatable illness; business and industry leaders who outrightly fire employees with a drinking problem instead of offering counseling, treatment, and rehabilitation; and people who cling to the mistaken notion that alcohol is the sole cause of alcoholism, may all be contributing, inadvertently or not, to alcohol problems."

Many societies use drugs of all sorts and seem to have no difficulty with them. Author Andrew Weil has pointed out rightly that the problems we have with drugs are not inherent in the drugs, but rather in our ways of thinking about them and about the states of consciousness people seek in them. The use of drugs to alter consciousness is not new; it has been a feature of human life in almost all places and in all ages. In fact, the only people who lack a traditional intoxicant, the Eskimos, had the misfortune to be unable to grow anything and had to wait for the white man to bring them alcohol.

"It is my belief," says Weil "that the desire to alter consciousness periodically is an innate, normal drive analogous to hunger or the sexual drive."[2] In drug-taking societies, he concludes, drug-induced states are not entered for negative reasons such as escape from boredom or anxiety. Rather, they are entered because they can be of positive usefulness to individuals and the tribe. This contrasts sharply with our practices. Too many people take drugs, including alcohol, for the wrong reasons—or for no reason at all—and this difference is what creates a drinking problem.

CHAPTER ONE

1. Margaret Culkin Banning, "Lit Ladies," *Harper's* Magazine, January 1930.
2. Frederick Lewis Allen, *Only Yesterday: An Informal History of the Nineteen Twenties* (New York: Harper & Brothers, 1931).
3. Joseph C. Rheingold, *The Fear of Being a Woman: A Theory of Maternal Destructiveness* (New York: Grune & Stratton, 1964), p. 480.
4. Bonnie-Jean Kimball, *The Alcoholic Woman's Mad, Mad World of Denial and Mind Games* (Center City, MN: Hazelden, 1978).
5. "Women Arrested for Drunk Driving in Boston," *Journal of Studies on Alcohol*, 37–5 (May 1976):648.

CHAPTER TWO

1. Mimi Ferlemann Barbara, "A Career Counselor Looks at the Devaluation of Women," *Menninger Perspective*, Winter 1977, p. 19.
2. "Women in the Labor Force: Some Mental Health Implications," *Psychiatric Opinion*, September 1979, pp. 17–19.
3. Sharon C. Wilsnack, "The Needs of the Female Drinker: Dependency, Power, or What?" Abstract reprinted from the proceed-

ings of the Second Annual Alcoholism Conference of the NIAAA.

4. John Langone, *Bombed, Buzzed, Smashed or . . . Sober: A Book About Alcohol* (New York: Avon/Little, Brown, 1979), pp. 52–53.

5. Edith S. Gomberg, "The Female Alcoholic," in *Alcoholism: Interdisciplinary Approaches to an Enduring Problem*, ed. by Ralph E. Tarter and A. Arthur Sugarman (Reading, MA: Addison-Wesley, 1976).

6. "Postmenopausal Promiscuity Often a Resurgence of Teen Behavior," *Ob. Gyn. News,* March 1, 1977.

7. John Langone, *Death Is a Noun* (Boston: Little, Brown, 1972), pp. 46–47.

8. *McCall's Magazine*, August 1978.

9. Jack Mendelson and Nancy Mello, "Biologic Concomitants of Alcoholism," *New England Journal of Medicine*, October 25, 1979, pp. 912–919.

10. John Langone, *Bombed, Buzzed, Smashed or . . . Sober*, pp. 176–177.

11. John Langone, "Why Do 'Reasonable' Students Take a Risk with Drugs?" *Sunday Boston Herald Traveler*, November 3, 1968, p. 6.

12. Georgi Lolli, "Relation Between Alcoholism and Specific Feminine Physiological Functions," *Connecticut Review on Alcohol*, 5–3(1953):9–11.

13. Margaret Culkin Banning, "Lit Ladies," *Harper's* Magazine, January 1930.

CHAPTER THREE

1. David L. Davies, "Definitional Issues in Alcoholism," in *Alcoholism: Interdisciplinary Approaches to an Enduring Problem*, ed. by Ralph E. Tarter and A. Arthur Sugarman (Reading, MA: Addison-Wesley, 1976).

2. Sharon C. Wilsnack, "Women Are Different: Overlooked Differences Among Women Drinkers," Keynote address, Symposium on Alcoholism and Women, Institute for the Study of Women in Transition, 1977.

3. Annie Gottlieb, "Risk Taking: Plunging into Life," *Working Woman*, April 1977.

4. Interview with authors, September 1979.

CHAPTER FOUR

1. Adelle Davis, "Why You Need Calcium," *Vitality Through Planned Nutrition*, Part 9, Bestways, May 1976.
2. Will Durant, *The Story of Civilization: Our Oriental Heritage* (New York: Simon & Schuster, 1954), p. 80.
3. "Alcohol–Acetaminophen Combination Can Be Dangerous," *The Journal*, July 1979, p. 5.
4. Sidney Gellis, "The Medicated Society," Lowell Lecture Series, February 14, 1967.
5. "Alcohol Exposure Goes to the Bones of Developing Fetus," *Medical World News*, August 6, 1979.
6. "Nursing Mothers Warned to Moderate Alcohol Intake," *Tufts–New England Medical Center News*, February 1979.
7. David Smith, "The Fetal Alcohol Syndrome," *Hospital Practice*, October 1979, pp. 121–128.

CHAPTER FIVE

1. Edith Robb, "Alcohol Victimizes Children Indirectly," *The Journal*, September 1, 1979, p. 12.
2. Claudia Black, "Children of Alcoholics," *Alcohol Health and Research World*, Fall 1979, pp. 23–27.
3. Interview with authors, September 1979.

CHAPTER SIX

1. Jeanne Marecek and Diane Kravetz, "Women and Mental Health: A Review of Feminist Change Efforts," *Psychiatry*, 40–3(November 1977):326.
2. Ruth Sanchez-Dirks, "Reflections on Family Violence," *Alcohol Health and Research World*, HEW Publication No. (ADM)70-151, 4–1(Fall 1979):14.
3. Nancy T., "Reaching the Lesbian Alcoholic," Paper presented at the Rutgers University Summer School of Alcohol Studies, June 1978.
4. "Alcoholism: Searching for Some Answers," *Menninger Perspective*, Winter-Spring 1979.
5. Interview with authors, September 1979.

6. Betty Ford, with Chris Chase, *The Times of My Life* (New York: Ballantine/Harper & Row, 1979), p. 307.
7. Harvey McConnell, "Sailors, Admirals, Celebrities Treated Equally at Navy Rehabilitation Center," *The Journal*, July 1, 1979.
8. Ronald J. Catanzaro, "The Evolution of Familization Therapy," undated publication of the Palm Beach Institute.
9. Carolyn Riley, "Institute Treats Entire Family," *West Palm Beach [FL] Sun-Sentinal*, June 20, 1977.
10. Interview with authors, September 1979.
11. *Journal of Studies on Alcohol*, March 1979.
12. Jean Kirkpatrick, *Turnabout: Help for a New Life* (New York: Doubleday, 1977).

CHAPTER SEVEN

1. Morris E. Chafetz, *Liquor: The Servant of Man* (Boston: Little, Brown, 1965).
2. Andrew Weil, *The Natural Mind* (Boston: Houghton Mifflin, 1972).

Index